Emigration and Social Change

Emigration and Social Change

A Sociological Study of the Early Emigrants of Andamans

ARVIND K. JOSHI

RAWAT PUBLICATIONS

Jaipur • New Delhi • Bangalore • Mumbai

ISBN 81-7033-929-4

Published by
Prem Rawat for *Rawat Publications*
Satyam Apts., Sector 3, Jawahar Nagar, Jaipur 302 004 (India)
Phone: 0141 265 1748 / 7006 Fax: 0141 265 1748
E-mail: info@rawatbooks.com
Website: www.rawatbooks.com

Delhi Office
4858/24, Ansari Road, Daryaganj, New Delhi 110 002
Phone: 011-23263290

Also at Bangalore and Mumbai

Typeset by Rawat Computers, Jaipur
Printed at Nice Printing Press, New Delhi

Dedicated to my Mother

Contents

Preface

For more than 50 years into Independence, it is a fact that the Andaman Islands are still the *Kala Pani* for most of the part of our country. It still does not enter into their perception that they form part of the country. This is also the feeling that the Andamanese have against the countrymen, who they usually refer to as mainlanders. Truly, the small fraction of the mainlanders who know about the place, think of it as a dangerous place inhabited by the naked aborigines.

The Andaman Islands were used by the British colonial government as a penal settlement from 1858. Hundreds of criminals, all life convicts, were banished to this settlement in the beginning. Later, some hard-core political prisoners were also sent here; although the practice relatively diminished and finally stopped as the country reached closer to Independence.

Due to several reasons, Britishers thought of closing down the settlement in between but the idea was dropped finally. A plan was chalked out to develop the penal settlement as a 'self-supporting community'. Criminals and their families were sent to live in the colony. Several facilities were provided to them for earning their livelihood. Meanwhile, the graph of political activities was also rising on the mainland. Many political prisoners during the 1930s were sent to the infamous

'Cellular Jail'. They continued their political activities here also and penetrated among the other local residents. When the government failed to control the unrest, it was compelled to give them the option to return. Almost all of them preferred to come back.

In March 1942, during World War II, the islands were occupied by the Japanese but they came again under the British control in October 1945, and soon after its status as a penal settlement ended.

At the close of the status of penal settlement, it was mostly the criminals or their progeny that remained behind. All of them formed a 'new society' under the most adverse circumstances of their time. They are generally called 'local born' or early emigrants as they or their ancestors were transported or reached here prior to 1947, that is, during the period of penal settlement. Those who came during subsequent years, after the islands were opened to all, are called 'new emigrants'.

The 'early emigrants' or 'local born' are in a minority now because of the large influx of population after Independence. But the locals are unique in the sense that their first generation was forcibly and completely cut from their culture and mooring and their offsprings scarcely had any contact with their roots. They have formed a new 'synthetic society'.

The present study is concerned with the description and analysis of the socio-economic and cultural pattern of the 'locals' who between themselves have a certain amount of ethnic consciousness and cultural identity. As would be discussed in the chapters that follow, the locals are the outcome of the British policy of colonisation of the Andaman Islands. While comparing the characteristics of the people who were imprisoned in the Andaman Islands and those Indians, who migrated to other British colonies as indentured labour, we notice a qualitative difference. The indentured labour to each of the other British colonies recruited in groups from some specific cultural area of India, thus carrying with them a part of their culture and linguistic milieu and thus they were able to develop a miniature cultural India in those British colonies. As far as the early migrants to Andaman Islands are concerned they were drawn from different parts of India and not significantly in good number from any specific linguistic region and, therefore, they were unable to recreating in the Andaman Islands any specific linguistic cultural form. People of different languages, religions, castes and classes had to amalgamate themselves to create a new community which, on the one hand, must have retained features of Indian social life, while at the same time does not represent any specific culture area. What was the process of the formation of a new community? What is the specific social form of the community? How does it resemble the parent culture from India? To what extent it differs from the culture of the mainland especially in matters of caste and joint family based society? What factors of unity do they show and how do they react to the other migrant inhabitants of that place? These are some of the basic questions that have motivated the author to take up the present study.

Every mature individual in professional life is aware of his indebtedness to many people who have stimulated and influenced his intellectual development. Ordinarily, these are unrecorded, except in author's prefaces or acknowledgements. First and the foremost, I wish to express my heartiest gratitude to late Prof. Gopal Singh Nepali who guided my research work with keen interest, scholarly advice and meticulous care. His style of research guidance rigorously followed the style of his own supervisor, late Prof. G.S. Ghurye. I am also thankful to Mrs. Nepali who always showered her motherly affection on me.

I am thankful to Prof. B.N. Juyal for his constant support and invaluable guidance from time to time on all aspects of the subject throughout the course of the work. My gratitude to him cannot be expressed in few lines. I am also thankful to Prof. Iqbal Narain, former Vice-Chancellor, BHU, for encouraging me to get this work published.

My gratitude goes to Prof. Y.B. Damle (Emeritus Professor, University of Pune), Prof. Yogendra Singh (Jawaharlal Nehru University, New Delhi), Prof. Baidyanath Saraswati (an eminent anthropologist), Prof. Anoop Chandola (Arizona University, USA), and Prof. Swapan Kumar Bhattacharya (Calcutta University, Kolkata) for bringing me back into the stimulating academic environment that has enabled me to complete this scholarly activity. Their gentle blend of prodding and encouragement ideally suited to keep me at work.

I have taken the assistance of many persons in the course of this study. But I would like to express my gratitude especially to late T.R. Pandey (then Principal, TTI, Port Blair), Mr. G.K. Nair (the then Rehabilitation Officer, A&N Islands), Mr. Ratan Singh Rayapa (the then Ecologist, ASI, Port Blair), Mr. R.C. Biswas, Mr. Gauri Shankar Pandey (the then Sr. Sanitary and Food Inspector, Port Blair), and my friends of Port Blair town Mr. Rajendra Lal, Mr. G. Narshimha Rao, Mr. P. Ahmed, Mr. Dennis Ajay, Mr. B. Lal, Mr. Raja Ram, Mr. Tamil Selvam, Mr. Dilip Kashyap, Mr. Pramod Paachpore, Mr. Rajesh 'Neerash' who helped me in many ways during my stay and field work at Port Blair.

I am thankful to the University Grants Commission, New Delhi for awarding me Junior Research Fellowship, otherwise it would have been difficult for me to carry on the fieldwork at Port Blair. During the survey of literature I have been largely benefited by the libraries of JNU, BHU, Sapru House, National Achieves, etc. My special thanks go to the staff of those libraries.

This work was originally done in Hindi. I am thankful to Prof. R.S. Sharma (former Head, Department of English, BHU, Varanasi) and Prof. P.K. Pandey (Department of English, BHU, Varanasi) for helping me in the English translation.

I would also like to express my gratitude to Dr. A.R. Prasad (Reader, Department of Economics, BHU, Varanasi) for making some extremely helpful suggestions that have greatly improved the final product. I deeply appreciate his help.

Finally, I take this opportunity to offer my deepest regards to my revered father, Mr. A.S. Joshi (former Deputy Registrar, Banaras Hindu University, Varanasi), and thanks to my wife, Dr. Vibha Joshi (Lecturer, Department of Economics, Vasanta College for Women, Rajghat, Varanasi). I would also wish to place on record my loving affection to my son Abhinav and daughter Apoorva who spared me from all parental obligations and kept me occupied with pen and paper. No words can express my feelings for them, and the sacrifices they have made. This token gesture is the least I can do.

At this important moment of my life, I wish to remember my mother late Krishna Rani Joshi who had always been an eternal source of inspiration and guidance to me. She has revitalised me at various stages of my academic pursuits. I wish she would have lived to see my work published!

List of Tables

1 The Andaman: Historical Development as a Penal Settlement

The Andaman and Nicobar Islands have figured as an issue in international politics during the last decade of the eighteenth century when the colonial government in India used them as a 'penal settlement'. The distant location amidst the deep sea of the Bay of Bengal and the torturous and barbarous treatment to the inmates by the jail authorities has made these islands as a symbol of terror in people's mind as *Kala Pani*. From the beginning of their rule in India, the British thought of establishing a penal settlement for criminals, beyond the sea far away from the mainland. They established the first penal settlement in Bencoolen in Sumatra beyond the sea on West Coast of Polembeng. They were till then using the Bencoolen for transportation of criminals from India – the first batch sent in 1787. The British had taken over the Bencoolen penal settlement in 1685 and renamed it as St. Marlborough.[1] In 1825, on the transfer of Sumatra to Dutch, such convicts were sent to Singapore and Penang in the Straits. Penal settlements were also opened for Indian convicts in Arracan and Tennesarim, the territories ceded to the British in 1826 by the Burmese ruler.[2]

Historically, the infamous penal system of 'banishment' was actually the cause of development of the Andaman as penal settlement. In the context of the present study, it will be useful to give a brief account of 'banishment' and then throw light on the colony's historical development.

Practice of Banishment

Under this penal system, prisoners are banished to prison colonies on foreign lands. In early days, criminals were mostly deported to far-off places in labour camps or on public work projects. In most European colonies, criminals would also be sold as bonded slaves.[3] Besides France, the practice of banishment of criminals was prevalent in Great Britain, Portugal, Spain, the Netherlands, Denmark and Russia but by the twelfth century most European countries had given it up.[4]

The first recorded incident of sending prisoners to a penal settlement is to be found in England during the reign of Charles II.[5] Until the eighteenth and early nineteenth century, there was also provision for banishment in lieu of capital punishment, Australia being the main destination for it. Several convicts who were banished went to New South Wales (called "Botany Bay" by the criminals) but since 1820 "Van Demen's Land" in present-day Tasmania became a major penal settlement. After 1840 sending prisoners to New South Wales was stopped and gradually during the years 1853 to 1864 the practice of banishment too was given up.

Banished prisoners were kept under strict military vigilance. A policy change was attempted in this regard during second half of the nineteenth century and some relaxation was given. In 1852, a prison code provision was made for the banishment of prisoners to India, East and West Africa.[6] After abolition of capital punishment in 1867, the number of banished prisoners swelled. In 1886, imprisonment was also coupled with banishment.[7]

In pre-revolution Russia, banishment was a common practice. Prisoners were deported to Siberia especially to work in silver mines of Nertchinsk.[8] Deportation of prisoners to colonies beyond the sea was not much resorted to in Spain. After the American Revolution, deportation of prisoners from England to America was stopped. Some prisoners were sent to Africa, but, not being able to withstand the hot climate, they perished. Then it was stopped. Banishment was still prevalent in the Soviet Union and prisoners were sent to labour camps in Siberia, east of the Ural.[9]

During their rule in India, the British exiled prisoners to the Andaman islands up to 1942. Between March 1942 and October 1945 the islands were under Japanese occupation. Subsequently, the British regained them, but as Indian independence was imminent, they finally stopped deporting prisoners to Andaman.

Geographical Position of the Andaman

The Andaman and Nicobar Islands are a part of the Indian Republic, located between 6°30' to 14° northern latitudes and 92° to 94° eastern longitudes. They are situated 950 kms away south-east of Hoogly in West Bengal, and 1,127 kms from Chennai, in the Bay of Bengal. The 10° and 145 kms wide waterway separates the Andaman and Nicobar Islands. The sea is 400 fathom deep. The total area of the Andaman is 6,408 sq kms and that of the Nicobar 1,841 sq kms. The headquarters is Port Blair, which is 1,191 kms from Chennai, 1,255 kms from Kolkata, and 1,200 kms from Vishakhapatanam.

Historical Existence of the Andaman

The people of South East Asia had known about the Andaman islands since time immemorial. On the basis of legends and folklore existence of the Andaman may be connected with tales in Sanskrit literature. People of Malaya referred to it as 'Handuman'. Actually, the Malayans pronounce 'Hanuman' of the Ramayan as 'Handuman'. In due course of time, it was simplified to become Andaman. We do not have any other details different from mythological literature. Historically, these conjectures are of comparatively lesser importance. Especially in the Ramayan, Hanuman is mainly related with Kishkindha region.[10] Portman too has doubted it.[11] According to him, perhaps, Andaman is derived from the name of Roman cartographer, Agasyodemin.[12]

From the second to sixteenth century different travelogues describe it as an island of cannibals. A famous second century geographer of Roman Empire in his world map mentioned some Agmate or Aginate islands in the Indian Ocean, probably referring to the Andaman, but Portman has refuted the inference.[13]

I'Tsing, a Chinese monk of sixth century, who visited these islands sometime between 671 to 673 AD, called them Andaman. He too has described its people as cannibals.[14] The Arab travellers of ninth century too say so.[15] The fact is that their description is based on legends.[16] Similarly, some have called them Angmanian[17], some Swarnadveep and some Andamania[18]. Travellers passing through here have described its people "with face like dogs", "cannibals"[19], very violent and terrfying[20].

It is not possible to authenticate narratives of different travellers. The authentic description begins from the mid-eighteenth century when commanders of East India Company and Royal British Navy started surveying the islands and submitting their reports.

Colonisation

Occupied by battles, empire expansion and consolidation by diplomacy in India, the East India Company did not pay much attention to these islands. By mid-eighteenth century, after capturing South India, the Company felt the necessity of having a port of refuge, as a surveillance post from naval point of view, in the Indian Ocean and the Bay of Bengal. John Ritchie who surveyed the Bay of Bengal in 1777 brought forth the importance of the Andaman islands.[21] Captain Thomas Forrest[22] in 1783 and Captain Buchanan[23] in 1788 drew the government's attention towards the need of again exploring the islands. Finally, in 1788, a survey team under Lt. Archibald Blair of Royal Indian Navy was sent there.

First Colony (1789-1796)

On the basis of Lt. Blair's report, in a council meeting of 12 June 1789, Governor General Lord Cornwallis decided to colonise the Andaman islands.[24] The main purpose was to find out a suitable, convenient and cheap port for British ships, which could be used as refuge from monsoon storms and as a safe place during wars.[25] Other secondary reasons for colonisation of the islands were: to save shipwreck passengers from violence of the natives and to control Malayan sea-pirates active in the Indian Ocean and the Andaman sea.[26] The decision of British Indian Government not to use Andamans as a penal settlement up to this point of time, is significant.[27]

A group of soldiers, labourers, and artisans under Blair reached the Andaman in September 1789. They landed on Chatham island on the south-east of Great Andaman (then called Port Cornwallis and now Port Blair) and established a residential colony. By August 1790 the total number of emigrants was 190.[28] Emigrants from Calcutta (Kolkata) on personal work were allowed to bring their families. In 1792, the total population rose to 360.

Blair was quite successful in making the residential colony of Chatham self-reliant but in November 1792 on suggestion of Commodore Cornwallis the colony was shifted to north-east corner of northern Andaman. The new place was named Port Cornwallis and the old one after Blair's name was christened Port Blair (until then known as Port Cornwallis).

On 5th November 1792, Captain Alexander Kyd was appointed as Superintendent of Andaman,[29] but he took over only on 5 March 1793; until then Blair continued as the Superintendent. One of the factors in the choice of the new place was its good climate. But, reaching Andaman, Kyd found many emigrants suffering from fever and bodyache.[30] Although several efforts were made to improve the situation, the problem got complicated. In the second half of 1793 many labourers, prisoners, and soldiers died. Suffering rose from the sudden onset of fever and weakness caused by splenalgia, most residents became invalid to work.[31] The monsoon was particularly severe in 1795, making majority of labourers, doctors and officers sick[32], during which more than fifty people died.[33] The hopeless condition lowered the morale of emigrants and they wanted to leave the island. On 4th February 1796, Captain Kyd appraised the Secretary to Governor General of the state of the emigrants.[34] On 8th February 1796, the Governor General's Council, keeping in view high incidence of sickness, increased death rate, exorbitant costs and difficulties involved in supplying essential commodities to the island, and in the interest of humanity and parsimony, decided to withdraw the decision to establish residential colonies in the Andamans.[35] By May 1796, the colony was fully vacated. At that time, there were 270 convicts and 550 free men, women, and children (including European officers and soldiers) in it. The prisoners were sent to Penang and rest to Bengal with their movable property.[36] Thus, the first effort to establish residential colony on Andamani soil by any outside authority failed.

Scheme Revived

It so happened that following cancellation of colonisation programme, many battle ships and merchant vessels were damaged in the Andaman Sea in 1796. The surviving passengers of shipwrecks had to take refuge on these islands and had to suffer inhuman conditions. Some fell victim to native's violence and some died of disease. On the night of November 11, 1844 two battleships the *Runneymede* and the *Briton* met with accident.[37] Again, in 1849, the *Emily* and the *Flying Fish* met the same fate near western Andaman. The natives climbed on *Emily* and killed an officer. Consequently, the British government once again thought over the scheme of building 'refuge' on these islands for passengers of shipwrecks.

The Board of Directors requested the Governor General to think afresh on the whole problem. At the same time, the Government of India was considering establishment of a penal settlement on south-west part of the islands for which its Secretary had sought advice from the government of provincial Bengal. The latter sent a letter to this effect to Henry Hopkinson, Commissioner of Arrakan.[38] Hopkinson agreed with Government of India's suggestion that the only effective and workable solution to the problem is establishment of a penal settlement on the island. The government was considering Hopkinson's letter when Maulemein's letter regarding murder of eight Chinese traders on the island reached.[39] After making a thorough study, the then Governor General, Lord Canning expressed his view against the proposal on the ground that, since certain territories in Singapore, Arrakan and Tenessarim were already being used as penal settlements, no new place was immediately required for the purpose.[40] Besides, unhealthy climate of the islands and the enormous expenditure involved on maintaining the colony also went against it. Although, Hopkinson had argued that putting prisoners to work could cut down expenditure, Lord Canning remained unconvinced, so much so that he did not give much weightage to strategic importance of the islands. In his view, British naval strength was so great that no foreign power would dare capture these islands for colonisation.[41] Hence, why establish military outpost at such a far-flung place, which despite a lot of expenditure would not be strong enough even to keep itself secure? The proposal to develop Andaman as port, refuge or residential colony was under consideration, when *gadar* (army rebellion) engulfed the whole country.

1857 Rebellion: Jail for Rebels

The British government was not the least concerned with life, welfare and moral of its myriad of subjects. "The company remained uninterested in anything other than import, export monopoly, salaries, profit and believed that its duty was to exploit India and not to civilise her."[42] A century of such misrule over India was bound to have terrible consequences engulfing the whole country in a conflagration or rebellion. The 1857 rebellion broke the illusion harboured by the British. The movement made it clear that, though one can rule by force over a subjugated people, loyalty cannot be procured by force.[43] However, lack of constructive ideology behind the rebellion resulted in its failure.

After the rebellion, came up an acute problem of keeping thousands of rebels sentenced for life in jail. The Government of India felt the necessity of taking a quick decision on penal settlement. Therefore, on November 20, 1857 'Andaman Committee' was constituted under Dr. Fedrick John Mouat with a view "to examine and select a suitable place on coasts of the Andaman groups of islands".[44] After making an in-depth survey, the committee submitted an intelligent and detailed report to Government of India.[45] Praising Blair for his contribution, the committee found the old port chosen by him as most suitable for a penal settlement.

Decision to Establish Penal Settlement

On the basis of recommendations of the Andaman Committee, the Governor General's Council decided that a penal settlement be built in the Andaman where prisoners sentenced for life or given banishment for crimes of *gadar* or rebellion and who cannot be sent to Straits settlement or to the Tenassarim Provinces be deported.[46] Thus, on the spot considered appropriate by Blair eighty years ago, building of penal settlement was started. The place was christened Port Blair after Blair's name. Captain H. Man was appointed superintendent of the penal settlement.[47]

Beginning of Penal Settlement in Port Blair

Captain Man was conferred total judicial and administrative powers over the Andaman islands.[48] He worked only for two months when a more experienced officer, James Pettison

Walker was sent as penal settlement superintendent. Walker reached there on March 10, 1858 along with four European officers and 733 criminals.[49] He made Ross Island his headquarters and it remained so up to 1942. In the beginning, he had to face many difficulties: prisoners' attempt to escape, native's attacks from time to time, and diseases, especially malaria, caused by the hot moist climate. Escapes, deaths in hospital or by hanging reduced the number of prisoners from 733 to 481.[50]

On October 3, 1859 Captain Haughton replaced Walker. His kind and considerate behaviour had desirable effect and the number of escapees came down. Besides, the prisoners realised that it is impossible to reach India, and escape meant death by starvation in the jungle or at the hands of the natives. Haughton was succeeded by Col. R.C. Tytler (1862-64) who also carried on a benign policy towards the prisoners.

Earlier, the Andaman penal settlement was directly under the Indian government, but in April 1864, its administration was transferred to Chief Commissioner of British Burma.[51] It was, however, realised soon that it did not bring about any improvement in administrative efficiency, rather mere correspondence between the superintendent and Indian government took a lot of time.[52] Therefore, in 1868, administration was once again transferred to the Indian government.

Convicts transported to Port Blair by the Government of India were either murderers who for some reason have escaped the death penalty, or perpetrators of the more heinous offences against the person and property. Their sentences are chiefly for life; but some, varying from very few to a considerable number, with long-term sentences, are also sent from time to time. Except those under 18 years of age but not over 40, and they must be certified as medically fit for hard labour before transportation. Youths between eighteen to twenty are kept in the boys' gang under special conditions.[53]

Regarding administration over prisoners, ample importance was given to their categorisation into different classes. It was believed that promotion to a better class would bring about improvement in a prisoner's character. This method was applied earlier by the British in 'Straits settlement' too. In the beginning, most prisoners were kept in 'class III'.[54] Those with good record and behaviour were promoted to class II after some time. These convicts worked as *Tindals* (warders) or *Sirdars* over other prisoners. Similarly, those with bad behaviour were demoted to class IV, as punishment. If class II prisoners worked well and their conduct was found satisfactory, they were promoted to class I. The first classers came under 'self-supporters' category and were given 'ticket-of-leave'. For making the entire colony self-supporting by encouraging cultivation and other technical skills, in 1858, Walker recommended 'self-supporter' and tickets-of-leave status to many prisoners (who had not even completed II and III class prison sentence)[55] but the government turned down the proposal.[56] After undergoing imprisonment for a specified period, class I prisoners were awarded clemency and put under self-supporter system in the Andaman penal settlement. The second class prisoners, who had completed three-fourths of their sentence without any record of bad conduct, were also given tickets-of-leave.[57] Those awarded self-supporter category were given financial assistance by the government for six months so that by then they could become self-reliant. Government would provide them land for agriculture along with help for poultry farming, animal husbandry, etc. If after a given period they were found unable to provide any profit to the colony, they were removed from self-supporter category and put again on 'gang work'. In May 1860, the Government of India issued orders to the Bengal government to despatch a small party of thirty female life convicts. An important change came about when in 1862, the government permitted the granting of 'self-supporter' status to female-prisoners too.[58] In 1867, it was decided that prisoners with weak health and above 45 years of age would not be sent to the Andaman. Arrangement for providing nutritious food to prisoners was also made. On experimental basis, 'mess system' was also introduced.[59]

In March 1868, Col. Man became the superintendent and in the same year, the Port Blair administration again went under the charge of Government of India. On April 16, 1869, British government captured the Nicobar islands. Another penal settlement was opened at Nancowry Port, which functioned up to 1888.[60]

The government made new efforts for prisoners' welfare and management of the colony. On the basis of suggestions[61] sent by Sir Henry Norman in this regard, the government made a revolutionary change in the prevailing slavery system for prisoners. It was agreed to set free life-sentence prisoners after 20 to 25 years under the clemancy system.[62] In 1876, a set of rules framed by Man and called the Andaman and Nicobar Regulations, was introduced to run the administration of penal settlement. In these rules, it was laid down that: "He who is sentenced to *Kala Pani* will have to work hard under strict discipline. He shall be given only that much of food which is essential for health. Anything more or any more facility will be considered kindness but that facility can be withdrawn partly or fully."

Prison population was increasing fast. Effective steps were taken to maintain the special character of, and discipline in the settlement. Policy level changes in the governance administration of Port Blair prisoners were also made. In January 1890, the Government of India sent C.J. Lyall and Lethbridge to the Andaman for consultation regarding prisoners' discipline and labour related problems. They submitted their report on April 26, 1890.[63] Their main finding was that, life-sentence prisoners prefer the Andaman penal settlement to Indian jails because in India life behind prison walls is comparatively harder. It was suggested that it was not proper to send short-term prisoners to Andaman. They were in favour of settling released prisoners in Andaman itself instead of sending them back to the mainland. In order to make punishment harsher, the report recommended that in the first stage the prisoner should be kept in isolation in a closed cell and in second stage confined to a limited area. It was also suggested to classify and grade habitual criminals from circumstantial criminals. In 1892, Superintendent, Col. Horsford began to implement these recommendations but they could be fully implemented only in 1894, when Col. Sir Richard Temple took over. Construction of the Cellular Jail, with a view to keeping prisoners under strict discipline began in 1896. It still remains unique and has now been turned into a national monument. It, therefore, deserves a brief description.

Cellular Jail

Although the entire Andaman and Nicobar Islands were turned into a prison colony, yet to handle law and order problems caused by an increasing number of prisoners, construction of a jail was considered necessary. Construction of the Cellular Jail was decided during Col. N.M. Horsford's tenure (1892-94), as Superintendent of Port Blair. The work was to begin from November 1893 but for unavoidable reasons it could begin only in 1896. The construction charge was given to sub-engineer Maeculen.[64] The estimated cost was Rs 5,17,352 but the total amount spent was only Rs 95,881. The rest came by way of prisoners' labour. The construction was completed in 1910 during Richard Temple's time, although there is a controversy in this regard.

In 1904, in a note, Superintendent W.R. Merk said: "Sending of prisoners to Andaman should be stopped because they, contrary to Indian prisons, have more freedom and comfort, except living for sometime in cellular jail."[65] He thought that such conditions were not conducive for 'reform' of the prisoners. Hence, sending prisoners to Andaman was sheer waste of government money. The Indian government after consulting state governments found that they were against total abolition of penal settlement.[66] In different Indian states, especially Bengal, an intense revolutionary movement was going on against the British. In 1910, political prisoners were again sent to Andaman. Hence, the Indian public became inquisitive about Andaman. The sheer objective of British government in sending political prisoners to such far off place was to stop them from spreading their revolutionary ideas among people and incite them for rebellion against the colonial rule.

Central and state governments were also worried about negative aspects of prisoners' rehabilitation in Andaman, e.g., prevalence of immoral practices and unfavourable health environment and it was being realised that the project could not be continued for long. But the main problem in abolishing the penal settlement was shortage of space in Indian prisons.[67] Hence, the government was compelled to prolong the project. Moreover, the rising tide of revolutionary activity in the first decade of the twentieth century forced the government to persist with it. As political prisoners from Bengal, Maharashtra, and other provinces were sent to Andaman, the Indian political leaders and intelligentsia became inquisitive about the conditions in Andaman. They demanded the constitution of a commission to examine administration of the scheme. Home Secretary, Reginald Credock too wrote about it to the government in his report after returning from Andaman.[68]

After the turmoil of First World War, the Government of India constituted a 'Jail Committee' under the chairmanship of Sir Alexander Cardew[69], which submitted its report in 1920. It termed prisoners' rehabilitation plan undesirable, unsuitable and expensive. It suggested that only hardened and habitual criminals should be sent to Andaman for safe imprisonment.[70]

Non-Cooperation Movement and Its Aftermath

The Non-Cooperation Movement under Mahatma Gandhi's leadership (1920-21) tremendously stirred the whole country. However, his method of non-violence did not convince many and as a reaction, revolutionary activities also thrived.[71] Indian jails were filled with political prisoners. Although on March 11, 1921, Home Secretary, Sir William Vincent had declared abolition of the penal settlement[72] and transportation of prisoners back to the mainland had also started. But the number was too large. Moreover, because of intense political activity and dearth of space in Indian prisons, the government was compelled to maintain the prison establishment of Andaman. Only female prisoners, political prisoners and prisoners under special crimes were stopped from being sent there.[73] Between 1920-23, during the superintendentship of Col. Beadon, about 1,400 rebel Mopala convicts from Malabar (Kerala) and some Punjabi prisoners were sent there. During Col. Ferrar's tenure (1923-31) many drastic changes took place. The idea of immediate vacation of the colony was dropped. A plan was chalked out to develop the penal settlement as a 'self-supporter community'.[74] Ex-criminals and their families were encouraged to live in the colony. In order to reduce pressure on Madras provincial jails it was decided to send Mopala Rebels to Andaman.[75] They were placed under the self-supporter category or employed in different departments. Those desirous of bringing their families were allowed to do so and given necessary facilities. These families settled down in different villages. Prisoners belonging to the criminal tribes, such as Bhantu of western UP, were also sent there on these conditions. Thus, in December 1926, in the prisoner population of 7,740, there were 2,105 self-supporters under government employment, besides 2,272 in agriculture.[76]

Provision of better facilities in the penal settlement resulted in increase in population. The proportion of women and children rose. Houses were built and provided on nominal rents. Restriction on coming to Port Blair was lifted. Schools, hospitals, primary health centres were opened in villages and complete freedom and help were given for building temples, mosques, churches and gurudwaras.[77]

In view of rising political activities, it was once again decided in 1932 to send political prisoners to Andaman[77] and keep them in Cellular Jail. In protest, the revolutionary activists went on hunger strike. The protest reached its climax in 1937 and the government was compelled to send them back to the mainland.

Japanese Occupation

In March 1942, the Japanese captured these islands and authority was assumed by the Japanese naval commandant. Right from the beginning, the Japanese faced food shortages on these islands. The situation worsened so much that by the end of August 1942, rice stock for local population ran out. To cope with the situation, they killed the old and those unable to work by shooting them down or throwing them into the sea. Only those were spared who could work for them. Many men, women and children died at the hands of the Japanese.[78] The Japanese felt that secret intelligence was being sent to the British from here. In order to find out British spies, they let loose a reign of terror, victimising mostly the English knowing people. About 1,300 people were forced to leave Andaman.[79] Arrival of Indian National Army in February 1944 somewhat improved the situation.[80] The period of the Japanese occupation was one of great economic, social and psychological tension, and the whole settlement community united because of Japanese terror. At the same, time there took place the greatest mixing of ethnic population. To some extent, the problem caused by diversity of castes and religions was ended. The Japanese encouraged agricultural activities in Andaman.

Abolition of Penal Settlement

In October, the 1945 British army again captured these islands and declared abolition of penal settlement. At government expense, prisoners and free citizens were sent to the mainland. As a result, whereas in 1941 the population was 21,316, in 1946 it came down to only 14,000. During the decade of 1941-51, population fell down by 8.28 per cent.

Although the penal settlement was abolished in 1945, the situation of Andaman was such that people were scared of going there. Besides, until 1947, comfortable transport facilities were not available. The terror of Andaman as *Kala Pani* on people's mind was such that it could be removed gradually only after the country's independence.

Andaman After Independence

When the Republic of India came into being, these islands were declared Union Territory and Port Blair was made the administrative headquarters. The administration of this Union Territory is headed by a Chief Commissioner (until November 11, 1982) and by a Lt. Governor since November 12, 1982, who under section 239 of Indian Constitution, administers the Union Territory under the direction of the President. Before independence and later up to July 31, 1974, Andaman and Nicobar group of islands formed one district. But later, they were separated, for revenue administration: (a) Andaman district under administrative control of Deputy Commissioner with headquarters at Port Blair, and (b) Nicobar district under administrative control of another Deputy Commissioner with headquarters at Car Nicobar. This Union Territory has no legislative body of its own. Up to 1967, the Member of Parliament representing this Union Territory was nominated by the President but since 1967 general election, the MP from here is elected directly by the people. A few years ago, a Regional Council was also constituted.

After independence, a large number of people have come here for permanent or temporary residence. During 1951-61, population growth rate was +105.19 per cent; many coming here from mainland India, in search of job or trade or to settle down here. Most of the emigrants are from Tamilnadu, Kerala and West Bengal, probably because these places are directly connected by sea route to Port Blair and people from these areas have already been living here. Whereas people of other states of India know little about these islands. The government too started settling refugees in different islands from 1949, the majority being Bengali refugees from East Bengal in the first phase. There is another important section of population, government officials, including officers of class one and two, who come here from mainland on deputation for a specific period. There is a larger number of class III government employees who are from the mainland. The proportion of locals has increased but they live apart from the rest.

Although the population can be classified in several sections according to their characteristics, the present study mainly focuses on those Indians who themselves or whose ancestors had settled down in Andaman before 1947, either voluntarily or on being transported here as convicts. In the study, other sections of population figure only as points of reference or comparison. No categorisation of the population has been made in the census reports as early emigrant, new emigrant or government officials, so much so that pre-1947 settlers or their descendants too, have not been categorised separately. Hence any estimate about the proportion of early and new emigrants is purely conjectural. The total population in 1971 was 1,15,133[83] out of which approximately 16.20 per cent was that of natives, 35 per cent of the population (approximately 40,000)[84] is of early emigrants, the remaining, that is, approximately 49 per cent of new emigrants, including government officials posted there. Obviously, the ratio of early emigrants in total population is comparatively small and it is gradually decreasing, since a large number of people from mainland India are coming every year to settle down here. Nonetheless, the "early emigrants" are a very significant group/subject for any study regarding "continuity and change". Moreover, they are also mobilising in order to protect their interests and demand preferential treatment in government employment, welfare schemes, and so on, and then try to acquire a distinct identity.

Notes

Though the author has consulted several books, reports and documents in the Library of National Archives in New Delhi yet the present chapter is mainly based on L.P. Mathur's book "History of the A&N Islands (1756-1966)", Sterling Publishers, Delhi, 1968.

1. Majumdar, R.C., Penal Settlement in Andamans, Gazetteers Unit, Department of Culture, Ministry of Education and Social Welfare, Government of India, New-Delhi, 1975, p.47.
2. Mathur, L.P., op. cit., p.130.
3. One such penal settlement of ill repute was located in the Devil's Island in French Guyana where Captain Alfred Dretpus was appointed incharge. *Collier's Encyclopaedia*, Vol. 7, William D. Halsey, Macmillan Educational Corporation, New York, 1977, p.470.
4. *Collier's Encyclopaedia*, Ibid., p.470.
5. *Everyman's Encyclopaedia*, Sixth Edition in Twelve Volumes, Edited by D.A. Girling, J.M. Dent & Sons Ltd., London, 1978, p.26.
6. *Encyclopaedia of the Social Sciences*, Volume Fifteen, The Macmillan Company, New York, 1957, p.91.
7. Ibid., p.91.
8. *Everyman's Encyclopaedia*, op. cit., p.26.
9. Ibid., p.26.
10. Sen, P. *Land and People of the Andamans*, Calcutta, 1962, p.5; Mathur, L.P. *History of the Andaman and Nicobar Islands*, Calcutta, 1968, pp. 6-7.
11. Portman, M.V., *A History of our Relations with the Andamanese*, London, 1899, Vol. I, p. 50.
12. Agathodaemon: Roman Cartographer and Mathematician of the 5th Century who drew the maps of the world in accordance with the explorations of Ptolemy.
13. Portman, M.V., op. cit., p.50.
14. Takakasu's Edition of I' Tsing, pp. 28-30 in Mathur, L.P., Ibid., p.7.
15. Pemberton *Collection of Voyages and Travels*, Vol. 7, p.183.
16. Mathur, L.P., op. cit, p.7.
17. Polo, Marco: A citizen of Venice who passed these Islands on his way to China (Started for China in 1260), in 1290, refers to these Islands as 'Angamanian'. He returned to Venice in 1295 and wrote an account

of his troubles and travels. Sykes' *A History of Exploration*, London, pp.66-83.

18. Nicolo Conti, who visited Andamans in 1440, mentions the Andaman Islands as 'Andamania' which he explains to mean as 'Island of Gold'. For details, Portman M.V., Ibid., Vol. I., p.53.
19. Priar Odoric: A European traveller who wandered over Asia passed Andamans in 1322 and called the people of Andaman Islands as dog faced and cannibals. For details, Sykes', Ibid.
20. For example: Cesare Federio, a European traveller, who touched the shores of Andamans in 1569, mentioned the ferocity of the Andamanese, Mathur, L.P., Ibid., p.8.
21. N.A.I., Home Department, Miscellaneous Volume, No.77, 1777, p.41.
22. Captain Thomas Forrest: N.A.I. Home Department, Public Branch, O.C., No. 43-44, 28 April 1783.
23. Captain Buchanan: N.A.I. Home Department, Public Branch O.C., No.30, 10 March 1788.
24. N.A.I., Secret Department, Progs, Volume, 12 June 1789 (O.C.No. not given).
25. N.A.I., Secret Department, Progs, Volume, No.6 to 29, 30 December 1789.
26. Mathur, L.P., op. cit., p.49.
27. Ibid., p.49.
28. N.A.I., Home Department, Public Branch, ABC, 22 September 1790.
29. N.A.I., Home Department, Public Branch, O.C.No.1, 5, November 1792.
30. N.A.I., Home Department, Public Branch, O.C.No.6-8, 27 March 1793.
31. N.A.I., Home Department, Public Branch, O.C.No.7-15, 7 October 1793.
32. N.A.I., Home Department, Public Branch, O.C.No.3, 13 July 1795.
33. Mathur, L.P., op. cit., p.57.
34. N.A.I., Home Department, Public Branch, O.C.No.1-3, 5 February 1796.
35. Ibid., No.5, 8 February 1796.
36. Ibid., O.C. No. 30, 23 May 1796.

37. The account of the Runneymede and Briton's Wreck was published in *Englishman*, a newspaper of Calcutta in 1845. It has been reproduced by Portman, M.V., at p. 156 in Vol. I of his book.
38. Arracan (a province in Burma), N.A.I., Home Department, Public Branch, O.C.N.82, dated 6 August 1858.
39. N.A.I., Home Department, Public Branch, O.C. No.83, 6 August 1858.
40. Ibid., No.79, 6 August 1858 (Minutes dated 15th March 1856).
41. Majumdar, R.C., op. cit., p.55.
42. Lt. Commandent Martin quoted by Tara Chand, *Bharatiya Swatantrata Andolan Ka Itihas*, Vol. II., 1969, Publication Division, New Delhi, p.93.
43. Tara Chand, op. cit., p.93.
44. N.A.I., Home Department, Judicial Branch, O.C.No.14-27, 15 January 1858.
45. N.A.I., Home Department, Judicial Branch, O.C.No.19, 15 January 1858.
46. Ibid., O.C. No.21, 15 January 1858.
47. Mathur, L.P., op. cit., p. 68. According to Mazumdar, R.C., op. cit., p. 62, in order to carry out the committees recommendations Govt. of India instructed Capt. H. Man, Executive Engineer and Superintendent of Convicts at Moulmein, to proceed to Port Blair and formally take possession of the Islands and arrange for the founding of the settlement. Captain Man proceeded to annex the Islands and made the Preliminary arrangements, but the establishment of the new settlement was actually carried out by Dr. J.P. Walker, who was appointed the first Superintendent of Port Blair.
48. Ibid., A Progs. No. 23, 15 January 1858.
49. Mathur, L.P., op. cit., p.132.
50. *Census of India, 1931*, Vol. II, Part I and II by M.C.C. Bonington, p.5.
51. Ibid., A Progs. No. 13, 1 April 1864.
52. N.A.I., Home Department, Public Branch, A Progs. No.224, December 1868.
53. *Imperial Gazetteer of India*, Vol. XX, Oxford: The Clarendon Press, 1908, p.196.
54. N.A.I., Home Department, Judicial Branch, A Progs., No.21, 15 January 1858.

55. N.A.I., Home Department, Judicial Branch, A Progs, No. 1-20, 29 July 1859 quoted by Mathur, L.P., op. cit., p. 150.
56. Ibid.
57. Ibid., A Progs. No. 7-23, July 1860.
58. Ibid., A Progs. No. 12-18, 16 July 1862.
59. Mathur, L.P., op. cit., p.137.
60. Mazumdar, R.C., op. cit., p.104.
61. N.A.I., Home Department, Port Blair Branch, A Progs. No.75, August 1874.
62. Ibid., A. Progs., No.80, August 1874.
63. N.A.I., Home Department, Port Blair Branch, A Progs. No. 74, June 1890.
64. Andaman and Nicobar Manual Settlement Order No. 423, Cellular Jail, Aberdeen, Port Blair, 13 September 1893.
65. N.A.I., Home Department, Port Blair Branch, A Progs, No.28-40, July 1906.
66. Ibid., A Progs. No. 28-40, July 1906.
67. Ibid., A Progs. No. 80-93, December 1910.
68. Ibid., A Progs. No. 34, April 1914.
69. Government of India, Home Department, Resolution No.63, Jails, 28, 1919.
70. Report of the Indian Jail Committee (1919-20) Para 563-566, pp. 285-286.
71. Mazumdar, R.C., op. cit., P.293.
72. Legislative Assembly Debates, 11 March 1921, pp. 956-60.
73. Legislative Council Progs. 17 January 1922.
74. Home Department, Resolution No.20/26 Jails, 27 February 1926.
75. Home Department, Resolution No. 188/24 Jails, 4 October 1926.
76. Home Department, Resolution No. 20/26 Jails, 27 February 1926.
77. *Census of India, 1931*, p.25.
78. Mazumdar, R.C., op. cit., p.294.
79. File No.601/7652/H. Ministry of Defence, Japanese Occupation of the Andamans, p.10.
80. *Census of India, 1951*, Vol. XVIII, "The Andaman and Nicobar Islands", p. xii.
81. File No. 601/7652/H-Ministry of Defence, Japanese Occupation of the Andamans, p.10.

82. Ibid., p.4.
83. *Census of India, 1971*, "A Portrait of Population: Andaman and Nicobar Islands", Series 23, M.C. Joshi, Director of Census Operation, Andaman and Nicobar Islands, p.59.
84. Information received from Mr. Sharda Ram, the then General Secretary of the 'Local Born Association', Andamans.

2 Theoretical Exposition and Methodology

As clarified in the previous chapter, the present study is about the society of banished Indians and their descendants in the Andaman, which came into being as a penal settlement. A popular Hindi proverb *Bhanumati ka Kunba*, meaning creating something from heterogeneous things taken from different sources applies aptly to the Andamanese society. In the early phase of its colonisation, people came here not out of their own volition, but after they were banished by the colonial government. Hence, their coming here was a form of punishment.

Curiosity should naturally arise as to how this society consisting of two very different kinds of people, that is, the high-spirited, self-sacrificing freedom fighters and hardened criminals, came into being. And such is the curiosity at root of this study, but it does not end here. Knowledge about Andaman society is important not only in the national context, but also as a subject of considerable theoretical importance, especially in the field of sociology. 'Immigrant society' has been one of important subjects of sociological research, especially in USA and global influence of American sociology in this area is well known.

Theoretical Exposition

In his preface to the classic work on human emigration, *The Uprooted,* Oscar Hindlin[1] writes: "Once I had thought of writing history of emigrants in America but then I found that the emigrant is actually history of America." Our canvas is pretty different but perhaps this statement applies to Andaman even more than America. Besides, this island really has no history other than the record of the 'convicts' deported here.

Regarding theoretical importance of problem for study, we may say that it represents a specific form of social change, and it is important both for historical understanding of dynamics of change as well as of sociological importance in discerning future direction of change.

During the seventeenth to nineteenth centuries, large-scale emigration from one continent to another took place mainly because of expansion of Europe and growth of imperialism and in the process several immigrant societies came into being such as USA, Canada, Latin America, South Africa, Australia, New Zealand, etc. Examples on small scale too can be given. In study of such societies cultural assimilation and evolution of a kind of 'hybrid' culture has been a major theme and to a great extent this is also the subject matter of present study. But no two émigré societies may simply be comparable wholly, and involved at the root are elements like cause of emigration, numbers, time and country, etc. It is necessary to look into these factors.

Dynamics of population movement has been causing social change. It has been and will remain an important factor of social change, economic development and political organisation.[2] History has been witness to migration of population from one place to another. In early times population movement was slow. Besides, it could be put in the category of conscious and purposeful emigration. This cannot be said about later emigration, much of which was caused by political upheavals.

History is witness to the fact that large-scale movement of population has contributed a lot to development of civilisation and social change. Scarcity of natural resources, famines or production failure caused large-scale population movement from one place to another that gave births to new nations, cultures, and political camps. Invasion, war, victory, and historically important penal process of banishment, also caused large-scale redistribution of population. Religious tyranny and narrow mindedness also drove thousands to leave their homes and go to safer places.

Thus, it is clear that every movement of population is not of the same nature. Causes of every population movement form an important basis for differentiation among such movements. Zivngmann and Ammende-Pflister[3] have divided movement factors as follows:

Physical

War and natural calamities like drought, famine, flood, climate, etc.

Economic

Unemployment, low standard of living, lack of social security, government action (such as displacement caused by construction of dams etc.), industrialisation and urbanisation, desire for high-level social security and benefits.

Social

Family troubles, residential and professional difficulties, children's future, inspiration and assurance from emigrant relations and friends.

Psychological

Individual conflict, desire to evade and run away from circumstances, restlessness, difficulty in harmonising with prevailing social condition, fear of war or punishment, attachment to other cultures and adventure.

Religious

Religious intolerance and desire for religious freedom.

Political

Discrimination, ill-treatment and political ambition.

Professional

Insufficient salary or gains, insufficient research facilities, etc.

None of the above factors of emigration apply fully to respondents of our study. We may place our respondents broadly under political in a special sub-category of "victims of administrative and political repression" which would include both 'political criminals', as well as ordinary criminals, who, in order to crush them, are sent to far off places. This also includes those who have been banished from the country or exiled.

Thus, images of two kinds of emigration came up clearly: voluntary and compulsory. Whatever the cause of population migration to a new environment it has to harmonise with the host society and in the process it has to adopt some elements of that society and to change or modify some of the migrants' own characteristics according to the requirements of host society. This process inevitably causes social change.

The historical context, conditions, number, and root cause of emigration are intimately related with social change, or we may say that it has important effect on structural and behavioural counter-form of society. We may divide social change into two forms as under:

(i) Voluntary Form of Social Change

When populations migrate to another place of its own will without any compulsion then the social change too is voluntary because the individual has freedom of choice of the place and opportunity.

(ii) Compulsory Form of Social Change

When people are sent to another place by force without caring for their feeling and desire or they are compelled to do so by natural or political upheavals, then the change generated by such migration is involuntary and often painful. This is nothing new whenever populations migrate from one region to another, particularly in cross-cultural settings, such diverse forms are clearly visible.

Whenever mobility increases because of industrialisation, urbanisation or any other factor, a new wave of migration in a new society takes place. There people of diverse castes, sub-castes, and of same caste settle down. This is a continuing process and therefore relevant for understanding the future direction of social change.

Thus, the sociological importance of present study is that it would help understanding the process of social change.

Objectives of the Study

Immigrant societies have been a subject of inter-disciplinary study in social sciences. USA has the most prosperous and powerful immigrant society. This has been a major subject in its diverse themes across several disciplines of Social Sciences: Sociology, Anthropology, Economics, Political Sciences, Social Psychology and History.

A major subject of sociological research has been how people uprooted from diverse cultural backgrounds (fragment cultures) created a new community transcending their respective narrow social circles. Similarly, forms and process of cultural assimilation have also been a major subject of study in what has been called the framework of harmony. How a new identity or social character was built. Relationship with local tribal communities too has been one of major subjects. The present study has the following objectives:

(1) To analyse historical development of early emigrant Andaman society.

(2) To analyse main socio-cultural characteristics of a 'synthetic society' made by people thrown in most unfavourable circumstances.
(3) How people with diverse characteristics through integration and self-reliance make a cohesive social system, and the factors that urge them to do so.
(4) How these diverse cultural groups are different from each other through their specific culture characteristics that they have received from their original cultural group.
(5) To what extent emigrants brought here during the initial phase of formation of the penal settlement have been able to maintain their mixed culture to the present time.
(6) What is the understanding of early emigrant group settled here in unfavourable circumstances before independence, of new emigrants arriving in large numbers after independence and competing for the resource and opportunities. What is the attitude of new emigrants towards the old ones and what is the effect of the two on each other.
(7) What theoretically important inferences can be drawn from this study as to the problems of social integration and adjustment.

Selection of 'Early Emigrants'

It was necessary to choose some of the most relevant community based on earlier study of structural features of Andaman society, in accordance with objectives of this study and within limited resources available. From this point of view, community of the descendants of prisoners sent there from the time of establishment to abolition of the penal settlement (administratively until 1947) seemed most important.

They represented a special type of compulsory emigration, where there is no significance of the individual's will and he is sent from one region to another by force and is compelled to settle there. They did not go to Andaman for any facility or opportunity and whatever be the reason, their number was very small. The main reason for taking 1947 as the dividing year is that India was dependent until then and whereas, on one hand, these islands were being used as a penal settlement, on the other hand, reaching there was not easy and people of mainland had a fear about the place. Curiosity about artificial society made by prisoners and their descendants is natural. Whereas from a researcher's point of view this group has a special appeal, from administrative point of view also it has been defined separately. Census report puts them under Andamani-Indian[4] or local born[5] category. The subjects of our study relate to this category. All respondents are members of this 'early emigrant' group. Although at places it discusses the effect of post-independence voluntary emigration on them or the changes occurring thereafter, this study however, throws light basically on early Indian emigrants.

Descriptive Hypotheses

The following hypotheses can be made in relation to the present study:

(1) If people of diverse socio-cultural characteristics, severed from their original society, are forced to huddle together at a particular place in unfavourable circumstance, the society that would be formed as a result, shall be devoid of the superior cultural traditions and collectively undergo cultural impoverishment in the process of evolution of a new cultural system.

(2) Circumstances of emigration and rehabilitation would further disintegrate structure of the group.

(3) Handing over work or occupation to people in a situation of compulsory emigration, under a plan or on random basis, would destroy the occupational basis of caste. Under such circumstances, the breaking up of the traditional caste-occupation fixity would at the same time, also undermine the traditional caste-based social hierarchical organisation.

(4) In such 'synthetic society' evolving in a new place, it would be feasible only for those to maintain their separate

identity, whose diverse necessities are fulfilled among themselves because of their sufficiency of number.

(5) If the immigrants use the same language in the new place, this may causes a language problem. The situation is further complicated when families speaking different languages arrive in small number from different places to settle down in one place. This situation gives birth to some 'mixed language' or pidgin language to communicate.

(6) When people of diverse religions, castes, sub-castes and language groups settle down in one place, especially under compulsive circumstances, the process of 'secularisation' may grow faster.

(7) In such a synthetic society the caste feeling is stronger among high castes in comparison to lower castes.

(8) High incidence of interreligious marriages may eliminate possibility of religious discrimination. The mass resident's attitude inclines towards secularism or at least religious tolerance.

Related Studies

It is significant that many studies have been made pertaining to native tribes of the Andaman and Nicobar like Ongi, Andamani, Nicobari, and Shompen (see W.H. Lig 1939; C. Boden, 1903; A.R. Redcliffe-Brown, 1922; E.H. Mann, 1933; D.N. Majumdar, 1958; L. Cipriyani, 1966, etc.). Yet on basis of survey of available literature in sociology and anthropology, it can be said that no systematic study has been made at least in these two disciplines on pre-independence 'early emigrants' society in Andaman. And this is the *raison d'etre* of this study.

A holistic approach has been adopted in this study. In early times, population settled mainly in Port Blair area in south Andaman. Therefore, for data collection Port Blair town where the early emigrants are mostly concentrated was chosen as the universe. The original primary data collection for the study was done in three phases through field visits to Port Blair: November 1979 – January 1980; November 1980 – January

1981; and 15 May 1981 – 31 May 1981. Afterwards, the author visited Port Blair and collected facts several times during 1992 to 2000.

Methodology

Before setting out to elaborate the research methodology, it seems necessary first to analyse the streams of emigration to Andaman in a historical context. Although, detailed account of it has been given in the first chapter, yet the main and relevant points are recapitulated here.

British officers had decided to colonise the Andaman Islands on June 12, 1789[6] but for unavoidable reasons the decision was rescinded on February 8, 1796.[7] The 1857 rebellion created grave problem of accommodating thousands of rebels in the Indian jails. Consequently, the decision was revived again in 1858.[8]

From 1858 to 1942, prisoners from all parts of India and Burma would be sent to the Andaman penal settlement. They were divided into two categories: first, those guilty of murder, dacoity or other heinous crimes and who for some reason escaping capital punishment were sentenced to life imprisonment and banishment; second, those banished to Andaman for rebelling against British rule or involvement in crime of political conspiracy. The latter were called political prisoners. In March 1942, the islands were captured by the Japanese. Numerous men, women and children died because of their tyranny.[9] In October 1945, the British recaptured these islands and thereafter penal settlement was finally abolished. The prisoners sent here during penal settlement period may be put in the category of compulsory emigration. On the other hand, people coming for different services or for trade and settle down may be kept under voluntary emigration category. However, their number was small. In 1947, when the country became independent, population emigrated to these islands on large-scale, because of displacement as a result of the country's partition, or in search for employment and business opportunities. Since 1949, the government also began settling emigrants and refugees, mainly from East Bengal, here under a rehabilitation programme. Even now thousands are emigrating every year.

In the context of the present study, it is necessary to clarify that it is based only on those Indians, who or whose ancestors were sent to or arrived in Andaman before 1947 and they have been called early emigrants. Sen[10] and Pandit[11] too have studied them under this category.

Seen theoretically, if people have to live in a new environment in which there is no scope of acclimatisation or adoption of some local social forms, drastic social change seems natural in the synthetic society made by diverse groups of people thrown together. A distinct possibility is that they will build such a society in which, keeping in view local condition and requirement, either different kinds of *taboos* and *sanskaras* are modified or done away with. In such a society, there would be little effect of traditional values, beliefs and ideas on individual behaviour. Different traditions related with family and marriage could change according to local requirements. Whereas, because of preponderance of various religions, caste and cultural groups and continuous inter-mixing among them, a process of secularisation has developed, but the process is not clearly discernible, because the ethnic and regional identities by origin, overlap.

Study Universe

The present study is confined to early emigrants in Port Blair town located in south-east part of Andaman. It is the largest town of Andaman and Nicobar Islands. The town is located with many functions: port works, administrative headquarters, trade, industry, and cultural centre of the entire Andaman. In other words, we may say that Port Blair is the administrative, trade and commercial capital of the Union Territory. Located amid hills, Port Blair is a clean attractive town with coconut trees growing at about sea level. The town's expanse on all sides is surrounded by bays, with pretty wooden houses, winding roads going up and down and breathtaking meeting and separation of land and the sea present a unique sight. For its nearby historical and natural spots, it is a centre of tourist attraction. The metropolitan character of the town with different people with their diverse cultural activities, enhance its attraction and give it specific flavour. Yet, the resources available for development in this territory are few and limited. Forest is the main natural resource. Other resources with potential for development are tourism, fishing and plantations, especially coconut and arecanut.

For the first time in the census in 1951 Port Blair, administrative headquarters of the Andaman and Nicobar, was treated as a 'urban' centre. In all earlier censuses it was taken as geographical area under which came many villages and the administrative headquarters in real sense was in Aberdeen, also in Port Blair.

Port Blair's population is increasing fast, mainly because of large number of people coming every year from the mainland. In 1981, total population of Port Blair was 49,634 which in 1991 became 74,955. Thus, the growth during 1981-1991 was 51.03 per cent. Sex ratio in the town's population is 1000:720 women, whereas in the islands the ratio per thousand men is 761 women. The lower ratio of women in the town is because most of the labour class, for want of adequate arrangement of living accommodation and employment, live without family. The town being the main educational centre of the islands has the highest literacy in the whole islands, that is more than 82 per cent. During the first phase of data collection, the literacy was around 62.36 per cent.

Sampling

In real life situation, it is not possible to collect information about a whole group separately[12], therefore, the method of representational sampling has to be chosen. "A statistical sampling is a miniature picture of the entire group or total from which sampling has been taken."[13] Since list of early emigrant families was not available, so the problem was which sampling method to use. Voters' list from Tehsildar's office was used for sampling. However, it was not possible to go to every voter's family to find out whether they were early or new emigrants. It is to be mentioned here that there are no house numbers. Therefore, it was decided at the outset that sufficient number of families be chosen. It was natural that when I went for data collection to chosen families, it was not necessary that these would be all members of early emigrant community. Some of them might be of new emigrant community and some families of high government officials coming on deputation for a specified period from the mainland.

I adopted random method of sampling from families mentioned in the voters list. Using "regular numbering system" of random sampling every tenth family was chosen for this study. Then a list of about 600 families was prepared for data collection. It is worth mentioning that when these families were contacted for data collection only 174 families were such whose head or ancestor had settled in Andaman before 1947. Therefore, it is obvious that attempt has been made to present a general picture of their community from data pertaining to different aspects of these 174 families and on the basis of views and attitudes of head of families.

Sampling always should be such that it represents properly the total study universe, so that reliable and authentic information may be gathered. An elementary problem before this researcher was – on what basis to prove that the chosen 174 families represent the early emigrant community of Port Blair town, which has a total number of 5,728 families. According to John M. Lobo, the then President of Local Born Association (the only organisation of early emigrants), there are about 1,750 families of early emigrants in Port Blair, which was also corroborated by an officer of Anthropological Survey of India. This means about 30 per cent of families residing in Port Blair are those of early emigrants. The data gathered by me for sampling also corroborates it. Thus, find that our sample is about 10 per cent early emigrant families with proper representation of every class and either group. The respondents consisted of 91.4 per cent men and 8.6 per cent women.

Sources of Data Collection

There are certain sources of reliable and relevant data in any study. Success of research actually depends on to what extent the researcher has succeeded in collecting actually reliable facts and information pertaining to his research subject. This depends on the reliability of sources of information. Thus, source of data is very important.

In the present study both primary and secondary sources of data have been used. Among secondary sources come books, records, government letters, survey reports, etc., and the primary sources are the direct respondents' families, community leaders and other knowledgeable persons.

Secondary or Recorded Sources

It was particularly borne in mind that before beginning the proposed research all related recorded sources were carefully studied.

Since no sociological study about the early Indian emigrants in Andaman has been made, the literature on their socio-cultural life is negligible. Although in pre-independence census reports, there is some information on this community. However, because of several factors, many changes have come since then. Besides, these reports cover only some aspects of the community. The researcher has collected related facts after making a thorough study of available books, articles, research papers and published news items on Andaman, irrespective of nature of these writings - historical, anthropological, geological, ecological (flora and fauna), memoirs or of any kind - all have been studied for the present research (bibliography on Andaman is given at the end).

Besides, public records too have been consulted. Thorough study of all old official data, information and orders housed in National Archive, New Delhi has been made and referred to in the course of study. Government files of different ministries too have been consulted. Facts from census reports, general administrative reports, and data published by government from time to time have been collected. Materials related to the study in different newspapers and magazines have been used according to requirement.

Data Collection from Primary Sources

Data collection has been completed in the following stages:

(1) First, field environment and concentration pattern of emigrant, etc., were studied by going to Port Blair town. Socio-economic and cultural life of the society was discussed with local knowledgeable people, which included early and new emigrants and high government officials on deputation from the mainland for a specific period.

(2) After getting acquainted with early emigrant society and its various aspects, an interview schedule was prepared which included both open and closed types of questions. No help from anyone has been brought for data collection through interview schedule. The researcher went personally to each respondent family to collect information by asking questions from the schedule. Head of each sample family was taken as the respondent.

Before giving a final shape to the interview schedule 30 respondents were interviewed for a 'pilot study' and pre-testing of the interview schedule. Every effort has been made while completing the interview schedule that the respondent had no feeling of distrust in his/her mind. It was only after informally talking over different topics that interested the respondent, and thus putting him/her at ease, that questions were put in between filling up of the interview schedule. One interview took on an average one and a half-hour. While interviewing for filling up the interview schedule, it was found that members of the early emigrant community were satisfied that at least one detailed and thorough sociological study was being made about of their community. Enlightened members of the community tried to give maximum information about their problems in the past or present and other important matters.

(3) In addition to interviewing family heads of the selected 174 families, some other persons referred to me as specially knowledgeable were also interviewed for getting information about history and other aspects of society. This included respected persons of early emigrant society, senior members, and people from different strata of new emigrant society. To understand different social problems, potentialities of development, different political and labour leaders and governments officials were interviewed in depth informally.

(4) Generally, interview situation is an artificial social situation in which both the interviewer and the respondent tend to take positions.[14] By becoming an active member and participating in activities of members of the group, vital information can be collected, as done by William White in his study Street Corner Society.[15] This researcher too, has successfully tried to do so during field visits. Following the participatory observation method, fully reliable and authentic information has been collected by taking part in different socio-cultural-religious and political activities of the society.

(5) An 'interview guide' containing a number of important questions was also prepared for data collection. It contained such questions or observational points, which were not thought fit to be included in the interview schedule. The data regarding many items on the interview guide were available to the researcher during participatory observation, yet for some questions help of specially

acknowledgeable members of the community was also taken.

Thus, an attempt has been made to analyse and collect information from primary and secondary sources on different aspects of history, demography, religions, linguistic origin and division, land ownership, economic pattern, caste and class hierarchy, education, occupation and employment, family, marriage and kinship, religious faiths and beliefs, festivals, *sanskaras* and superstitions, family and collective behaviour, such as participation in socio-religious festivals.

Case Study

In order to generate authentic data regarding different aspects like marriage, divorce, caste, untouchability and religious discrimination, magic and totem, etc., the case study method was also adopted.

Classification and Tabulation of Collected Data

The large amount of scattered materials collected from diverse sources has been classified in different categories on the basis of their similarity and dissimilarity. Keeping in mind the nature and objectives of the study, classification of data has been made on periodical, quantitative and qualitative basis. Under qualitative classification both differential and multi-quality kinds have been restored to. The main objective of classification has only been that analysis and interpretation became easy and accurate conclusions were arrived at.

A scheme of coding was devised for transforming the data from the interview schedule to the master charts. Thus, the tabulation was completed through 'hand tabulation system'. It may be mentioned here that "tabulation is considered a part of technical process of analysis of statistical facts[16]".

Analysis and Interpretation of Data

After arranging collected data through tabulation and classification, they were analysed and interpreted in historical context so that scientific form could be given to the study. Although statistical method has been used in the study wherever applicable, no tests of significance were considered fit to be used. The researcher has tried his best to make proper analysis and interpretation of data. It is said that authenticity of analysis mostly depends on researcher's general knowledge, experience, past knowledge and intellectual honesty.[17] The researcher does not deem it proper to say anything himself in this regard.

Limitations

Keeping in view the limitations of time and resources, the researcher was per force confined to the objectives of his study. We do not have facts regarding diverse topics like the socio-economic, cultural patterns of the communities from which people were banished or went to Andamans voluntarily, what was their state then and now, what was their original socio-cultural status, etc. Although some data have been collected from secondary sources yet it is difficult to say how far they were reliable, or representative. During 1943, the Japanese burnt all government records kept in the office of Chief Commissioner, Andaman.[18] Hence, vital information was lost. But whatever information, facts, and data are available have been used in this study.

Some Experiences of Fieldwork

Some problems, like establishing contact with respondents, are common in fieldwork that every researcher has to face. In the present study during data collection phase although all respondents cooperated fully, yet much time was lost in contacting some. In the evenings because of widely prevalent drinking habit they were not inclined, or steady enough to give interview properly. For fieldwork, daytime on holidays proved the best, but this also prolonged the process.

Although every attempt was made to ask questions from interview schedule as politely and informally as possible, sometimes owing to little knowledge of English or Hindi, the meaning of the questions was misunderstood and the interviewees (especially Mopala respondents) responded with vehement retorts. Local friends with knowledge of two or three languages cooperated in the study by working as interpreters.

Many respondents being over-conscious tried to suppress facts regarding questions on income. However, the researcher was successful in collecting authentic information indirectly. During first phase of data collection many respondents did not give information regarding their other houses and rental incomes. During the second and third phase of data collection, the researcher, however, could gather information from the respondents about their house-ownership and income from rent. Similarly, information gathered about drinking habits, caste origin, etc., was also cross-checked through talking with one about another informally.

Notes

1. Hindlin, Oscar; *The Uprooted*; Grosset and Dunlop, New York, 1951.
2. Jackson, J.A., *Migration*, Cambridge University Press, 1969, p.1.
3. Zwingmann, C.A. and Ammende-Pflister, M. *Uprooted and After*, Springer-Verlag, New York, 1978, p.1
4. *Census of India, 1951*, Vol. XVII, "The Andaman and Nicobar Islands'" Appendix A, by Sri S.K. Gupta, p. XLIV.
5. *Census of India, 1901.*
6. N.A.I., Secret Department, Progs. Vol. 12, June, 1789 (O.C. No. not given).
7. N.A.I., Home Department, Public Branch, February, 1796 (O.C. No. 5, 8).
8. N.A.I., Home Department, Judicial Branch, January, 1858 (O.C. No. 15, 21).
9. *Census of India, 1951*, Vol. XVIII, "The Andaman Nicobar Island's", p. xii.
10. Sen, P.K., *Land and People of the Andaman's*, The Postgraduate Book Mart, Calcutta, p.77.

11. Pandit, T.N. "The Ethnic Situation in the Bay Islands", in *Yojana*, Vol.XX/13, 15 August, 1976, New Delhi, p.99.
12. Mann, Peter H., *Methods of Sociological Enquiry*, Oxford, Basil Blackwell, 1968, p.102.
13. Young, P.V., *Scientific Social Surveys and Research*, Asia Publishing House, Bombay, 1960, p.302.
14. Madge, J., *The Tools of Social Sciences*, Longmans, London, 1953, p.131.
15. Whyte, William, *Street Corner Society*, University of Chicago Press, 1949.
16. Jahoda, et al. *Research Methods in Social Relations*, Henry Holt and Company, Inc., 1959, p.270.
17. American Marketing Society, *The Technique of Marketing Research*, McGraw Hill Book Co., New York, 1937, p.283.
18. *Indian Historical Record Commission Proceedings*, December 1951, Vol. XXVIII, Part I, p. 113.

3 Social Pattern

The main objective of the present chapter is to analyse the social pattern of the society formed by people from different culture, caste, linguistic and regional backgrounds. The hierarchical form of the new social pattern is very clear. Since in census reports population has not been divided into early and new emigrant categories, it is not possible to have a comparative view of the two with regard to rate of population growth. We would assume that the people who settled before 1947 are early emigrants (excluding native tribes). The general features of the whole population are being presented here with the help of secondary source data. On the other hand, the study group has also been portrayed on the basis of data collected from primary sources.

During the early period of the penal settlement, increase or decrease in population were mainly determined by the governments sending or returning prisoners. Natural population growth began only after the government gave permission to bring families from the mainland or to marry local women. The population had increased at a fast pace since March 1942, but with the occupation of the Japanese forces it decreased rapidly. In 1945, when the British decided to abolish the colony, the population decreased once again because many people utilised the opportunity to go back to the mainland. After independence, the door was opened for large-scale emigration to Andaman. Every year thousands are emigrating to the islands for different purposes. Table 3.1 gives the rate of population growth in Andaman and Nicobar (including the tribes) from 1901 to 2001.

The table clarifies that during 1941-1951, population decreased because of deaths caused by tyranny of the Japanese and after abolition of the colony inevitable return of population to mainland. Thereafter, the high rate of population growth is surprising, especially during 1951 to 1961, but this influx has little to do with the early emigrants. Some of them may also have returned. A considerable portion of this belongs to the tribes of Andaman and Nicobar. The native tribes had no linkages with rest of the society as they lived in jungles in isolation. Therefore, in the analysis of trends of demographic change the tribes inclusion does not seem appropriate.

Table 3.1

Population Growth in the Andaman and Nicobar Islands

Census Year	*Population*	*Decade Variations*	*Decade Population Growth Rate (%)*
1901	24,649	-	-
1911	26,459	+1,810	+7.34
1921	27,086	+627	+2.37
1931	29,463	+2,377	+8.78
1941	33,768	+4,305	+14.61
1951	30,971	-2,797	- 8.28
1961	63,548	+32,577	+105.19
1971	1,15,133	+51,585	+81.17
1981	1,88,741	+73,608	+63.35
1991	2,80,661	+91,920	+48.70
2001*	3,56,265	+75,604	+47.55

* Provisional Population Tables: India, Part-I, *Census of India*, 2001.

The early emigrants settled mainly in south Andaman. Therefore, it seems necessary to make census-based analysis of Andaman's population from early years of penal settlement to its abolition, i.e., from 1881 to 1951. Available evidences shows that proportion of females in the population was very low. Increase or decrease in population was very slow. In 1941, the population was at its highest and in 1951 because of Japanese occupation and return of many, it came down to just 18,961.[1]

Table 3.2

Andaman Population, 1881-1951

Year	*Male*	*Female*	*Total*	*Decade Variation*
1881	12,940	1,988	14,628	–
1891	13,375	2,234	15,609	+981
1901	15,158	2,980	18,935	+3,329
1911	14,737	2,904	17,641	-1,297
1921	15,551	2,263	17,819	+178
1931	14,258	4,965	19,223	-1,404
1941	14,872	6,444	21,316	+2,093
1951	12,734	6,227	18,961	-2,355

On analysing population growth rate of the study area of Port Blair town, it becomes clear that the 1951 population (the year in which it was classified as a town area) was merely 7,789. It almost doubled to 14,075 in 1961 and took a quantum jump to 49,632 in 1971. In the total population, 28,855 were male and 20,777 female.[2] During 1951 to 1961, population growth was 55.3 per cent and during 1961 to 1971, 86.29 per cent and by 1981 it grew by 89.3 per cent. Obviously the population of Port Blair town is increasing very fast. According to 2001 census, the population of Port Blair town is 100,186 in which 55,507 are males and rest of the 44,697 are females.[3]

General Population Characteristics

This includes analysis of available census data according to religion, sex and language, etc. Before 1881, Andaman was not included in Indian census. During early period of Andaman, penal settlement the population was just 738 but it was not classified according to religions or language groups. First, we analyse the population in the historical context according to religion.

Population According to Religion

If the population is analysed under this head from early times to the present the following facts come out: the proportion of Hindus in the population decreased continuously from 1901 to 1941, whereas in 1901 their percentage was 37.58, in 1941 it came down to 25.96. Excepting for the census decade 1921, Muslim population has been increasing. In 1901, their percentage was 17.07 which in 1941 increased to 23.70 per cent. The proportion of Christian population came down only in the census decade, 1921-1931, otherwise it recorded an increase during 1901 to 1941. Whereas in 1901, their percentage was mere 1.97, in 1941 it rose to 7.74 per cent. In 1901, the followers of Jainism were just 0.25 per cent, which became extinct later on. During 1911 to 1941, there was not a single follower of Jainism recorded in the colony. Similarly, the number of Sikhs was very small. In 1901, their percentage was 1.50, in 1911 – 1.72, in 1921 – 1.44, then increasing gradually to become 2.20 during 1931 to 1941. It should be noted here that during 1901 to 1941 increase or decrease in population was according to rise and fall of penal settlement population. It is often heard that during British rule some prisoners embraced Christianity in order to escape from repression. Census of India, 1941 clearly shows the percentage variation of Christian population.

To analyse pre-1941 Andaman population, the 1941 census report will have to be taken as the base because this is the only best reliable source in this connection. The 1941 census report makes it clear that after tribes, the largest percentage of population is that of Hindus (24.95) followed by Muslims (23.70), Buddhist (8.59), Indian Christians (3.05), Sikhs (2.20), Anglo-Indians (0.29) and rest of religions (4.38).

Table 3.3
Christian Population – Percentage Variation

	Percentage Variation				
	1931-1941	*1921-1931*	*1911-1921*	*1901-1911*	*1901-1941*
India	+5.9	+32.7	+22.7	+32.1	+127.6
Andaman and Nicobar Islands	+78.9	?7.9	+180.2	+16.5	+437.7

Table 3.4
Foreign Emigrants[4]

Country	*1901*	*1911*	*1921*	*1931*
Nepal	9	14	10	3
Afghanistan	32	34	9	-
China	1	35	428	179
Japan	-	-	3	135
Other European Countries	2	1	6	3
Africa	1	-	1	3
America	3	3	5	3
Australia	-	2	15	8
Total	48	89	477	334

The above data show that contemporary population had representation of all religions. Obviously followers of different religions represented different Indian states. Besides these Indians, there were also foreign emigrants in local population which is shown in Table 3.4.

The table shows that in 1921 foreign emigrants were in the largest number. In total population, the immigrant's percentage has been very low. Besides these foreign immigrants, there were many immigrants from the British Islands (but in census report, specific islands are not mentioned) whose number was as follows:

Table 3.5

Emigrants of British Islands

Sex	1901	1911	1921	1931
Male	177	163	121	133
Female	13	18	12	12
Total	190	181	133	145

After independence, large number of new emigrants arrived in the island, whose population increased as follows: 30,971 in 1951; 63,548 in 1961. During 1961 to 1971, population increased by 81.17 per cent, the total population being 1,15,133, out of which 60.92 per cent were Hindus, 10.12 per cent Muslims, 26.35 per cent Christians, 0.75 Sikhs, 0.09 per cent Buddhist, 0.01 per cent Jains, 1.10 per cent other religions and 0.66 per cent did not tell their religion.[5] According to the latest available census data (1991), the break-up of population of Andaman and Nicobar Islands by major religions in percentage is as follows:

Table 3.6

Religion-wise Population of Andaman and Nicobar Islands, 1991

Religion	Per cent
Hindu	67.53
Muslim	7.61
Christian	23.95
Sikhs	0.48
Buddhist	0.11
Jains	0.01
Others	0.09
Religion not stated	0.22

Religion is considered a very private matter. Generally, people do not talk about or discuss religion in the streets. Followers of all religions live amicably and participate in each other's festivals, so much so that some would celebrate festivals of other religions, too, for example, a Muslim or Christian playing colours in Holi or participating in preparations for *Saraswati Pooja* or celebrating *Rakshabandhan* festival. Hindu boys may be found going to church or mosque. Generally, no controversy or conflict arise in the name of religion. On *Muharram* festival shias recite *marsia* in which at times Sunnis are also invited and they go, too. I came across some such Muslims who did not know their sect. Many years ago tension between two Muslim sects was heard. Earlier too, there were isolated instances but they should be treated as an exception only.

In the Andaman, the population has fluctuated between 1901 and 1941 as the strength of the penal settlement increased or decreased. But by 1941 the number of free settlers (including convicts who had elected to remain in these islands after completion of their terms and their children) increased. Facts reveal that just before Japanese occupation the population of the Andamans was the highest in March 1942. Variation in the natural population between 1931 and 1951 can be seen from Table 3.7.

Table 3.7

Variation in Natural Population (Andaman and Nicobar)

	1951				1931			
Percentage Increase (+)/Decrease (–) in Natural Population	*Recorded Population*	*Immigrants*	*Emigrants*	*Natural Population*	*Recorded Population*	*Immigrants*	*Emigrants*	*Natural Population*
+23.3	30,971	11,648	104	19,427	29,463	14,255	552	15,760

Population According to Sex

It is a significant fact that the available data for period 1874 to 2001, that is from the days of penal settlement to the present, shows that in Andaman the number of women has been much less than that of men. But it is also important that difference in sex ratio before 1926 was only because of the special condition in which only male prisoners were exiled here. In 1926, the prison policy was changed and prisoners were allowed to bring their families from mainland[6] resulting in rapid increase in female ratio. However, it remained much less than males. During 1874 to 2001, the male-female ratio is shown in Table 3.8.

Table 3.8

Sex Ratio of Andaman and Nicobar Islands

Year	*Male*	*Female*
1874	1000	130.8
1881	1000	132.6
1891	1000	141.6
1901	1000	130.2
1911	1000	352.0
1921	1000	302.6
1931	1000	495.4
1941	1000	573.7
1951	1000	625.3
1961	1000	616.8
1971	1000	644.1
1981	1000	761.2
1991	1000	818.0
2001	1000	846.0

Because of the peculiar character of the colony, in the beginning the sex ratio in the population was bound to be different. Although, female ratio increases after 1926, it still remained unnatural. After independence, the difference in sex ratio should have come down, yet majority labour emigration was an impediment because, the labourers preferred to leave their families behind in their native place. With the implementation of the government's plan to develop residential settlements in central and north Andaman, it is expected that the marked imbalance in male-female ratio would be corrected to a significant extent.

Marital Status Ratio

In 1921, married people were more than unmarried, but in 1951 the ratio was reversed. In 1921, there were only 303 female for every 1000 males. Looking at such wide difference in sex ratio it can be said that in 1921 majority of emigrants was prisoners transported here without their families, even if married.

Table 3.9

Marital Status of Male and Female Ratio per Thousand

		Census Year			
A&N		*1951*	*1941*	*1931*	*1921*
	Unmarried	564	–	448	365
Male	Married	396	–	481	549
	Widower	40	–	71	86
	Unmarried	512	–	439	405
Female	Married	394	–	490	462
	Widower	94	–	71	133

The data on marital status is not available for Port Blair town. Therefore, we are analysing on the basis of the data available for Andaman and Nicobar Islands.

These islands did not have the custom of child marriage. No one below 14 years was married. Only 0.02 per cent of women of this age group were married. Most of married male was of fecundating age group, from 15 to 34 years old and some of 35 to 54 years. Actually only these two age groups comprised the total married population.[7]

The primary data collection for this study was done during 1980s, therefore we are discussing here on the basis of the data that was available during that period. In comparison to 1951, the percentage of married population rose in 1961 to about 43.9 per cent. In 1971, it decreased slightly to 42.8 per cent. The 1961 and 1971 the status of married population is presented in Table 3.10.[8]

Table 3.10

Married Population of Andaman and Nicobar Islands

	Census Year	
	1961	*1971*
Total Population of the Islands	63548	115133
Total Married Population	27923	49346
(a) Male	17522	39287
(b) Female	10401	19059
Total Divorcee or Separated	387	539
(a) Male	251	360
(b) Female	136	179

Linguistic Composition

In Andaman and Nicobar Islands, the three main languages spoken in 1991 were Bengali (no. of speakers 64,706), Tamil (no. of speakers 53,536), and Hindi (no. of speakers 49,469). Per cent wise they are 23.1, 19.1 and 17.6, respectively. Rest of the population speaks different languages like Telugu, Malyalam, etc. Presence of people from different provinces is proved by analysis of the respondents' mother tongue itself. Though in early census report data on the basis of native language are not available yet it seems more proper to analyse them in the present context during primary data collection period instead of historical perspective. On analysing population of this study area that is, Port Blair town, on linguistic basis, we find that the largest part is that of Tamil (5,693), followed by Hindi (5,455), Malayalam (5,096), Telegu (4,361), Bangla (2,064) and Urdu (1,977). Percentage-wise this comes to Tamil 21.7, Hindi 20.8, Malayalam 19.4, Telegu 16.6, Bengali 7.8 and Urdu 7.5. The remaining population speaks other languages. This total population consists only of early and new emigrants and tribes. If only early emigrants are to be studied on linguistic basis, then only the data collected from respondents will have to be taken as the basis because in census reports, there is no such division.

As for the respondents to the study, we find that 82.2 per cent speak Hindi/Hindustani in their homes, followed by Urdu 4.6 per cent, Bengali 2.3 per cent, Tamil 1.1 per cent, and Malayalam 9.8 per cent.

Thus, most of early emigrants speak Hindi/Hindustani in their homes. This linguistic classification of Hindustani is not researcher's own, but as mentioned by most respondents from that society. It is to be noted here that during penal settlement period when speakers of different languages interacted a mixed dialect was formed which they called Hindustani language. The 1951 census report also calls *lingua franca* 'Hindustani'.[9] The 1908 gazetteer also mentions Urdu/Hindustani language.[10] Some have called it Andamani Hindi. Sir Richard Temple has called it 'hybrid Urdu' containing in part words from English, Urdu and some according to local needs and situations.[11] It may be noted that most people who received education during colonial period knew Urdu rather than Hindi.

According to this researcher, the local language may be called mixed Hindi which attaches no importance to grammatical rules, particularly in the use of masculine and feminine gender. For example, a girl would say "*Hum jata*" instead of grammatically correct "*Main ja rahi hun*". Some other dialectal expressions are as follows with correct forms given in parenthesis: "*Usi log naraz hote honge* (*Ve log naraz ho rahe honge*); "*Hum kuch nahin karane sakata* (*Hum kuch nahin kar *sakate*); "*Kaman par jane se bolo*" (*Kam karane chalana ho to kaho*). This is the lingua franca. Many believe that this language developed because of large-scale emigration of different linguistic groups. In early times this was not the speech pattern. Although, 4.6 per cent of respondents have mentioned Urdu as their mother tongue, during study, it was found that most homes actually used mixed Hindi. However, elderly respondents did have some knowledge of Urdu. We find that in the earlier variety of Hindustani, there were many Urdu words. Most respondents, speaking Malayalam in their homes, had come from Mopala Muslim families of Malabar.

We do not find any feeling of superiority or inferiority on the linguistic basis, nor do we get any controversy in historical context. However, at present internal tension between Tamil, Bengali and Telugu-speaking groups may be seen, which is actually because of competition for rights and opportunities.

More socio-cultural interaction is to be found among same linguistic groups. However, no feeling of ill-will or inferiority and superiority towards other language speaking groups or persons is generally to be found. However, among the larger groups of early emigrants, awareness towards their native language has increased.

Though, the early emigrants form one broad social category within it, actually there are certain cultural groups, which largely confine their socio-cultural interaction within the group; and because they had arrived here in larger number from the mainland, they have been able to maintain their cultural identity to some extent. They are actually known by their specific ethnic names and may be identified as follows:

(1) Mopala group
(2) Ranchi (tribal) group from Chhotanagpur
(3) Bhantu group
(4) Anglo-Indian group
(5) Others or/the entire early emigrant group is called 'local born' in local language

Mopala Group

They are Muslims from coastal Malabar, which formed part of Madras Province during the British rule, and is in Kerala State at present. A great controversy exists regarding their origin, about which one can find information from books and articles.[12]

Because of Mopala uprising in 1921, no less than 1,400 Mopalas were sent here as prisoners. In 1929, some Mopala prisoners and free emigrants were also brought through their willingness from mainland for good. In 1931, there were 1,885 Mopalas in Andaman.[13] During early years of penal settlement these Mopalas were assigned to clear forests, build the *gymkhana maidan* and approach road to South Andaman colony. At present, most of them are engaged in agriculture or trade.

Most of them belong to Irnad, Valuvanad, and to some degree Calicut in south Malabar on the mainland. Because of coming here in groups, they have fully maintained their religion and culture. Moreover, during the early years, the villages in which they settled were named after their native villages in South Malabar, like Calicut, Vandur, Trirur, Majari, Malapuram, Manarghat, etc. Mopalas are easily distinguishable by their dress and dialect. There is not much of change in their traditional dress, which for men is *lungi* (which they call *mundu*), vest, a long shirt with 'U' cut bottom, a cap like *safa* (turban) and a pair of sandals. Most of the conservatives have shaven heads and faces. Mopala women wear a peculiar dress, identifiable from a distance. They wear polka dot chintz mundu, waist long or longer blouse. They do not practice *pardah*, yet cover their head with a white or coloured piece of cloth (*makkana*). They also wear silver or gilat (an alloy) waisteband (*aranyalu*). Their language, slightly different from Malayalam, is called Mopala Malayalam.

With reference to the study area that is, Port Blair town, their number is rather small. They are mainly settled longitudinally on both sides of the road, in Lilipur settlement of Phoenix Bay and Haddo area. They are mostly in service, or catch fish, or are engaged in agriculture or small trade.

Ranchi (Tribal) Group

In the early phase of this penal settlement, some tribals from the Chhotanagpur plateaus in Bihar were brought here as labourers to clear forests. Since they came from the place Ranchi, and since they actually belonged to that tribal region, they are called simply Ranchi. They are also addressed as *sathu*. These tribal peasants were sent here in large numbers. In the early phase, they were mostly placed in forest regions of South Andaman, far from Port Blair. After abolition of penal settlement and dawn of independence, a settlement comprising of service class Ranchi people came up in Port Blair town, near the Dairy Farm and Haddo area in a place called *kumhra kheti*. Ranchi folks are mainly labourers and they too, have maintained their cultural identity. They are mostly Hindus, but there are also numerous Christians. They practice black magic and totem. The particular intoxicating drink they prepare from rice called handia, is known to all here. By nature, they are simple and labourious. If their girls are married in some other caste or religion, they generally do not object, perhaps because of their relative backwardness.

Bhantu Group[14]

Originally named Dravid Bhantu, they came from a so-called criminal tribe of the then Central Province, whom the government have for long been trying to rehabilitate. In 1926, a large number of them were dispatched to penal settlement, a majority of them being life prisoners. They were put on agriculture in Andaman. Their number was small from the very beginning. In 1931, their number in Andaman was 91 male, 92 female, 59 boys and 43 girls totalling 285. Besides agriculture some young men, boys and girls worked as labourers in mills or other industries.

Tracing their origin to Chauhan Thakur dynasty of Chittorgarh they mainly worship *Devi*. They are divided among 22 *gotras*. Most of them consider themselves low caste Hindus but they neither go to Hindu temples nor invite Brahmin priest to any ritual or festival. Many of them have got converted to other religions after marriage and now besides Hindus, there are also Christian and Muslim Bhantus. Their traditions and customs remain the same but great change has taken place in educated families, who now even hesitate to call themselves Bhantus.

In the Bhantu settlements in Port Blair town no deprivation is seen. Some families are settled in Junglee Ghat area. Most of their settlement is in Cattleganj, far-off the town.

Anglo-Indians

Their percentage is nominal in early emigrant population. Their ancestors came here for service from the mainland during penal settlement time. Some of them are Anglo-Burmese. They are economically better off. Their main occupation is service. They also have large pig and poultry farms giving pretty good income. They command special respect among Christian. Though small in number their living style and customs and manners have some influence on local Christians. After them educated Christian families try to adopt English language and Englishness. They live aloof from the rest of early emigrant society. However, their marital alliances have taken place with early emigrants of other religions. Their emigration is not centralised at any particular place. Some families live in South Point area of the town and Aberdeen near municipal board and in Gole Ghar near Church Line.

The remaining emigrants includes all others excepting Bhantu Mopala, Ranchi and Anglo-Indians. Although representing different religions, languages and provinces and despite observing different customs, manners and rituals they clearly form a general group. There has been much marital mixing among them. Their general spoken language is mixed Hindi. "We feeling" is found to a great extent in them. Their main occupation is service and they are economically better off. Most of them own sufficient agricultural land.

Their settlement is all around Port Blair town mostly in Aberdeen Bazar, Aberdeen village, South Point, Phoenix Bay, Shadipur, Naya Gaon, Junglee Ghat, Lamba line, School line, Dairy farm, etc. A large number of them also lives in villages. It may be noted here that the British policy was to settle people of all religions, provinces and languages in a mixed manner and not separately, yet settlement pattern at this point of time shows some clustering of families of the same socio-cultural origin at the locality level. This is because of distribution of residential plots to them by government after Independence. Usually people of a settlement have greater feeling of belongingness toward people of their own settlement.

Original Residence Province

It is clear now that early emigrants hail from different Indian provinces of mainland. If analysed in totality respondents are mainly from UP (23.6%), followed by Kerala (21.8%), and West Bengal (8.6%). A not insignificant 6.3 per cent of respondents do not know about their native place and mostly represent third generation from penal settlement period. The data on native place of early emigrant population, however, shows that it represents almost all provinces as shown in Table 3.11.

The following facts emerge from information regarding the first member of family coming to Andaman: for the largest number of respondents' (40.3%) father had come first, followed by those (29.3%) whose grandfather had come first, and in 8.4 per cent cases it was the respondents themselves. In about 6.9 per cent cases, the great grandfather came first. Paternal, maternal, uncle, brother, maternal grandfather, father's paternal uncle of remaining 4.1 per cent respondents came next and 1.1 per cent respondents were such who did not know which ancestor had come first. They thought that possibly during early days of penal settlement someone of the family came who might have been the great grandfather.

Table 3.11

Distribution of Respondents According to their Native State

State	*Frequency*	*Per cent*
Uttar Pradesh	41	23.6
Kerala	38	21.8
West Bengal	15	8.6
Bangladesh	12	6.9
Tamilnadu and Andhra Pradesh (each 9)	18	10.3
Maharashtra and Punjab (each 8)	16	9.2
Rajasthan, Orrisa, Karnataka, West Pakistan and Gujarat (each 2)	10	5.7
Bihar	5	2.9
Burma	4	2.4
MP	3	1.7
Goa	1	0.6
Don't know	11	6.3
Total	174	100.0

Under what circumstances the original family member came to Andaman is important because it could throw light on whose descendants present generation of the early emigrant society are. Ancestors of most of early emigrants have been prisoners sentenced for crimes like murder, dacoity, etc. This is corroborated by the fact that ancestors of most respondents (74.7%), banished from the country on account of different heinous crimes were transported to this place as shown in Table 3.12.

Organisational Arrangement

The early emigrant community, mostly the descendants of the prisoners transported to this penal settlement, have been

Table 3.12
The Form of Emigration to Andaman

Who/In What Form	*To Settle*	*Prison-ers*	*To Study*	*Politi-cal Prison-ers*	*In Search of Job*	*Trade*	*Army Transfer*	*Tour-ing*	*Brought by Japanese*	*Abscond-ed*	*Not Known*	*Total*
(1)	*(2)*	*(3)*	*(4)*	*(5)*	*(6)*	*(7)*	*(8)*	*(9)*	*(10)*	*(11)*	*(12)*	*(13)*
Self	2 (6.3)	14 (43.7)	1 (3.1)	–	7 (21.9)	1 (3.1)	–	4 (12.5)	1 (3.1)	2 (6.3)	–	32 (18.4)
Father	1 (1.4)	56 (80.0)	–	–	5 (7.1)	4 (5.7)	9 (1.4)	1 (1.4)	1 (1.4)	1 (1.4)	–	70 (40.3)
Grandfather	–	43 (84.4)	–	5 (9.8)	–	2 (3.9)	–	–	–	1 (1.9)	–	51 (29.3)
Grandfather of Father	–	11 (91.7)	–	–	–	1 (8.3)	–	–	–	–	–	12(6.9)
Maternanal Uncle	–	2 (100.0)	–	–	–	–	–	–	–	–	–	2(1.1)
Brother	–	–	–	–	2 (100.0)	–	–	–	–	–	–	2(1.1)
Mother's Father	–	1 (100.0)	–	–	–	–	–	–	–	–	–	1(0.6)
Father's Uncle	–	1 (100.0)	–	–	–	–	–	–	–	–	–	1(0.6)
Uncle	–	1 (100.0)	–	–	–	–	–	–	–	–	–	1(0.6)
Unknown	–	1 (100.0)	–	–	–	–	–	–	–	–	1(50.0)	2(1.1)

Note: Figures in parentheses, denote percentage

looked down upon since the very beginning. It is mentioned that Indian officers hated them first because they were descendants of criminals and secondly because by the social standards they would not strictly observe the traditional norms specially while establishing matrimonial alliance.

On Colonel Beadon's (1920-23) advice, the 'local borns', mainly descendants of the convicts, organised themselves under Andaman Indian Organisation with a gazetted officer as president. The organisation worked for securing rights and welfare of this community. Even now an organisation of early emigrants, Local Born Association, is fully active, which accepts membership of only those who themselves or whose ancestors had settled here before 1942. It seems to be a non-sectarian organisation because it includes people of all religions, languages, and provincial origin. The organisation is mainly active for protecting economic interests of the members. Its members or early emigrants are not mixing well with new emigrants of their own religion or language.

Every year, a large population is emigrating to these islands. The increasing number of new emigrants has reduced early emigrants into a minority. They find a threat to their rights and existence on account of increasing rate of emigration. Under such an unfavourable situation, the Local Born Association is trying to protect rights and interests of early emigrants. The organisation has fought strongly from time to time on important issues like providing maximum job opportunities to its members, providing proper arrangement for education on mainland, and for agricultural and residential land from government and has succeeded to a great extent in securing the benefits from the government.

Members of early emigrant community are given preference in appointment to class III and class IV posts. In fact, most of these posts are fully reserved for them. This also includes those who were rehabilitated by government or have received five years of school education on these islands. People with five years of schooling in these islands are kept under 'local' category, which was opposed by the Local Born Association because children of high government officials on deputation from mainland also come under this category and derive all benefits. Some years ago, a rule was framed that he who has received continuous school education for ten years on the islands would come under category of local.

The Local Born Association is much dissatisfied on account of Andaman Special Allowance. Government employees on deputation from mainland and people selected for government jobs on the islands from mainland get 33.3 per cent of basic salary as Andaman Special Allowance. On November 28, 1980 the Local Born Association demanded from the Prime Minister of India that in the interest of equality this should be given to all.[15]

On August 20, 1980, the Association took out a massive rally of about 15,000 persons, led by its then president, John M. Lobo and secretary Sharda Ram, throughout the town in support of early emigrants' rights. Their demands were: repression of local people should stop; local unemployed be provided employment; they be given priority in government jobs; and stopping entry of outsiders in the islands in view of the reduced employment opportunities. The demonstration has been compared with the Assam agitation.[16] However, association members have vehemently opposed such comparison on the ground that they do not demand expulsion of people from the islands; rather they opposed new emigration.

It is said that a certain Congress(I) leader of the islands incited new Tamil speaking emigrants by spreading rumours that "They want to oust Tamilians from the island".[17] And in such an explosive situation Education Department changed timings of Tamil and Hindi classes in Haddo High School leading to tension between two groups and on September 4, 1980 violent conflict took place. Many students and members of public were injured and many had to be hospitalised. Central

Reserve Police was called to control the situation and Section 144 imposed.

On September 24, 1980, the Tamil-speaking people took out a procession under the leadership of a wing of D.M.K. – Tamil Education Protection Committee – against the 20th August Local Born Association procession and the 4th September incident. They demanded equal provision of land and opportunity for education and employment to all Indians without any preference being given to any class, group or place of birth.

This shows that a wide gulf has been created between new Tamil-speaking emigrants and early emigrants. This state of inner conflict may prove injurious to the future of Andaman. Strong feeling of regionalism is growing up in Andamanese society, even among early emigrants. The feeling of regionalism, so and so is from UP and so and so from Tamilnadu, etc., is motivating people to confine themselves to people from their own region. Some problems are cropping up because of conflict of interest and cultural identity, between early and new emigrants. The early emigrants claiming to be a 'homogeneous community' allege that new emigrants have created a cleavage in their community. In this connection it is to be noted that the Local Born Association had given a memorandum to State Reorganisation Commission requesting it not to settle East Bengal refugees here because this would cause break-down of homogeneous community.[18]

Along with new emigrants, Local Born Association is also unhappy with administrative officers on deputation from the mainland. A common joke about officials who generally come on a three-year deputation is that they spend the first year in sight-seeing, the second year is spent by them in settling down and in the third year they collect souvenirs.[19] It is alleged that there is no link between the people and the administration and neglect the islands completely. On the other hand, these officers also look at them with feelings of suspicion and contempt, so much so that the prosperous business class of early emigrant community also keeps itself aloof from them. Some people even though they belong to the community do not consider themselves to be its members because they consider it against their prestige. Persons coming from outside try to keep away from this society. Whenever, this researcher visited Andaman for data collection and met any high government official, he found him denigrating this society. Most of these officers would not let their children play with the children of early emigrants and believe that criminal blood of prisoners may any time incite the criminal instinct. But, the fact is that crime rate on the island is comparatively very low. On the other hand, early emigrants say that only competent and educated persons from their own society should be appointed to high government posts. They argue that the local would understand their problem better then the officials from mainland. Their argument is by the time the officer fully understands his job situations, his deputation would end and he would be transferred.[20]

On April 4, 1981 a delegation of Local Born Association met Chief Secretary for land reservation. They were informed that the Home Ministry has made the following provisions:

(a) 50 per cent reservation for members of pre-1942 emigrant families and for those who were brought here as refugee or emigrant under colonisation or rehabilitation schemes;
(b) 20 per cent for tribes;
(c) 10 per cent for central government employees; and
(d) 20 per cent for others in Locals category who have had ten years of continuous schooling on the islands.

In conclusion, we may say that the population of the Andaman penal settlement of yesteryears has increased manifold. It came down during Japanese occupation but after Independence it increased fast on account of various reasons like emigration in search of employment or other economic opportunities and rehabilitation by government. The population of the island increased by 81.17 per cent during 1961 to 1971. During the same decade population of Port Blair town increased by 86.29 per cent and during the decade, i.e., 1971 to 1981, by 89.3 per cent. Right from the beginning the ratio of female population in the colony was very low. Undoubtedly, the wide gap in sex ratio had deeper consequence. From the very beginning, the number of Hindus was the largest. At present in Port Blair town the largest number is that of Tamil speaking people followed by Hindi, Malayali, Telugu and Bangala speaking people. So far as respondents from early emigrant society are concerned, most of them speak Hindi or Hindustani at home, which is also their general conversational language.

Early emigrant population has many cultural groups like Mopala, Bhantu, Ranchi, etc. The largest groups have been able to preserve their cultural characteristics. In this sense they have a cultural identity. Generally, families with similar cultural characteristics have settled in small groups in a particular place. Majority of early emigrants under study are originally from UP followed by Kerala, West Bengal, Bangladesh, etc. For the majority of respondent it is their second generation here. It was their father who had been deported here. All early emigrants have tried to organise themselves under one banner. Whereas this organisation consists of people of diverse religious and linguistic groups, its main objective is to work for safeguarding the rights and economic interests of its members and in this sense the organisation is purely secular. Its members keep themselves away from new emigrants even with similar cultural characteristics and most do not try to unite with them. On the one hand, a large number of people are emigrating to the islands and on the other, employment opportunities are very few. That is why a situation of conflict is building between early and new emigrants.

Notes

1. *Census of India, 1951*, Volume XVII, "The Andaman and Nicobar Islands", Appendix A, p. XLIII.
2. "The Light of Andamans", *Weekly Newspaper, Port Blair*, April 13, 1981, p.4.
3. Provisional Population Totals: India, Part-I, *Census of India, 2001.*
4. *Census of India, 1931*, Vol. I, Part I-Report.
5. *Census of India, 1971*, Series I-India, p.2 of 1971-Religion.
6. *Census of India, 1951*, Vol., XVII, "The Andaman and Nicobar Islands", p. XXXIII.
7. Ibid., p. 5.
8. Basic Statistics Andaman and Nicobar Islands, 1979-80, p.45.
9. *Census of India, 1951*, p. XLIV.
10. *The Imperial Gazetteer of India*, Vol. XX, Oxford: The Clarendon Press, 1908, p.200.
11. Sir Richard Temple in *The Census of India, 1901.*
12. For Further readings see, "The Mappillas of Malabar" in *Marriage and the Family in Kerala*, Fr. J. Puthenkalam S.J., Journal of Comparative Family Studies, The University of Calgary, Canada, 1977; Hitchocock, R.H., *The History of the Malabar Rebellion*, 'Madras, Government Press, 1925; Abbas, M.H., *All About Khilafat*, a collection of speeches and writings related to the movement, Bombay, 1923; Tarachand, *Influence of Islam on Indian Culture*, Allahabad, Indian Press, 1936; Hamid Ali, *The Moplah, Malabar and Its Folk*, edited by T.K. Gopal Panikkar, 3rd edn., Madras, G.A. Natesan and Co., 1920; Mayer, Adrian, C., *Land and Society in Malabar*, Oxford University Press, 1952; Miller, Ronald E., *Mappile Muslims of Kerala*, New Delhi, Orient Longman, 1976; Abdulla, V., "The Moplahs", article in *The Illustrated Weekly of India*, Bombay, 1 February, 1970; Bannings, J.J., "The Moplah Rebellion of 1921", article in *The Moslem World*, XIII (1923), pp. 317-89, etc.
13. *Census of India, 1931*, p.26.
14. For details see, *Census of India, 1931*, Vol. II, Appendix-I, "The Bhantus", pp. 41-50.
15. "The Light of Andamans", *Weekly Newspaper, Port Blair*, March 2, 1981, p.5.
16. Rajendra Pal Sharma, "Assam Type Stir Grips Andamans", *Blitz*, November 8, 1980.

17. Ibid.
18. Sen, P.K., *Land and People of the Andamans*, The Post-graduate Book Mart, Kolkata, 1962, p.114.
19. Mukherjee, Mihir, "Andamans Still a Penal Colony", in *The Statesman*, July 10, 1980.
20. "Personnel Policy: The Multiple Horns of A Dilemma", in *Yojana*, Vol. XX/13, August 15, 1976, p. 46.

4 Caste System

The study begins with two hypotheses concerning caste: (a) that in a 'synthetic society' built anywhere, the feelings and practice of casteism are prevalent more among fragments of higher castes as compared to those from lower ones; and (b) that in a situation of forced emigration, because of random system of allotment of work, the occupational basis of caste will be destroyed. In new and adverse conditions traditional caste occupations would disintegrate and, at the same time, such disintegration would knock down the traditional hierarchical structure. Here, study of caste is more relevant because all early emigrants, not excluding the non-Hindus, even had originated from a society (mainland India) where caste was the basic element of the social system. It is often found that emigrant groups from India settling abroad have tried to maintain their caste system in new places also. In such a situation, the caste element moving from one place to another transforms itself in what may be called a dynamic form of caste. Here, it is necessary to mention that such social practice was feasible only when these emigrants settled abroad in groups. So far as the early emigrant society of Andaman is concerned, as clarified in earlier chapters, the individuals from different parts of India sentenced to banishment were compelled to live in this inaccessible place. Some homogeneous groups like Mopala, Ranchi, Bhantu, etc., were sent in groups. Description of the form of caste system in Andaman from beginning to the present is given in subsequent sections.

'Caste' is an important institution in Indian society. Caste system has been deeply influencing Indian life for thousands of years. Religions claiming total equality like Christianity and Islam too have not remained untouched by it. According to the census report of 1991, there are 94 caste groups among Muslims and likewise among Christians also there are divisions of high and low status groups, who maintain social distance from each other. The 1931 census enumerated 2,993 castes and sub-castes in India. Apparently, this was not exhaustive: according to Ghurye in every linguistic region of India there are about 2,000 castes.[1] While classifying both structural and institutional aspects of the caste system, Ghurye[2] described the following six characteristics:

Segmental Division of Society

Caste system has divided Hindu society in different segments. In each segment, the social position of its members creates in them fellow-caste awareness of their mutual responsibility and caste rules. A society bound by caste traditions has limited community feeling and instead of sense of moral duty towards the whole community, it is towards one's own caste. Every segment has its own judicial council, which may be called 'caste panchayat' – it dispenses justice in different disputes and punishes those who break caste rules.

Hierarchy

The social position of each caste is higher or lower in relation to another caste. Caste position is based on birth. In the Hindu caste hierarchy, Brahmins come at top followed by Kshatriya, Vaishya, and the untouchables. Each caste has different sub-castes with a definite hierarchical position.

Restrictions on Feeding and Social Intercourse

One caste is not allowed to drink water or eat food prepared by other castes. Caste rules clarify from whom members of a particular caste can eat food; *phalahari*, *kuccha* and *pukka* or take water. The most severe restriction is in relation to the untouchables.

Civil (Social) and Religious Disabilities and Privilege of Different Castes

Brahmins have the greatest privileges and untouchables the greatest disqualifications. The latter have to live outside or on the margins of village settlement. They could neither enter temples, nor go to school, or take water from wells or ponds of *savarnas* (high castes). They could not even go to main streets. Even their shadows were considered as inauspicious and polluting. They had no social or religious rights. Great changes have now taken place in the modern time.

Lack of Unrestricted Choice of Occupation

Almost every caste has a traditional and hereditary occupation and every one has moral and religious liability to earn his livelihood through his caste occupation. Occupations too have a hierarchy.

Restrictions on Marriage

Each caste has several marriage restrictions. No one is allowed to marry outside his caste or sub-caste. But marriage within ones own *gotra, pravar* or *pinda* is prohibited. These restrictions are generally applicable in one geographical and linguistic region. Marital alliance cannot ordinarily be made in different geo-linguistic regions; even within the same caste.

All characteristics of caste are to be found in the above analysis. In the present context, an attempt is made to trace the caste system in the emigrant society from penal settlement time to the present. Although scanty facts are available from secondary sources, yet whatever it is, on its basis it can be said that the caste system existed in these islands from the beginning till now in the following form.

Attempt has been made to find information about the caste of all Hindu respondents in this study. Generally, people do not talk about their caste when asked. Most Hindus say that their caste is Hindu or Hindustani. It is to be noted in this connection that 38.5 per cent of the 96 Hindu respondents did not exactly know their caste. However, some of them originally belonged to schedule castes and not mentioning it implies that even now they understand social position or hierarchical role of caste. Generally speaking, the respondents displayed that people are curious about their neighbours caste and also to mention it to any outsider. This interest in the caste of others makes it clear that people are curious about caste origin. All Hindu respondents analysed on caste basis:

Expression of ignorance about their caste origin by about 40 per cent of the respondents, and disinterest by most of the remaining about their caste background suggest that caste has no place as a significant social category in this society. It is also significant that only few respondents have mentioned caste of their wives. Out of these, one Kurmi has an Ahir wife, one Ahir has a Brahmin wife, two Uttar Pradesh Brahmins have Gujarati wives, one Reddy has a Bengali Kayastha wife, one Kayastha has a Brahmin wife, one Halwai has a Brahmin wife, one Kshatriya has a Brahmin wife, one Nayar has a Bengali Natha wife, one Ahir has a Nayadu wife, one Reddy has a schedule caste wife, one Kumhar has a Marathi Kshatriya wife, two Brahmins have Kshatriya wives, one Kshatriya has a Kayastha wife, one Marathi Rao has a UP Agrawal wife and one Brahmin has a Sunni Muslim wife. Thus, it is clear that in matrimonial alliances there is neither endogamy, nor has the usual linguistic limitation; and even inter-religious marriages are not treated as an aberration.

The British officers took special care of caste affinities and attitudes of the inmates of the penal settlement and made every effort to maintain it. The prisoners would be sent to Andaman penal settlement in ships. During the sea voyage and later in prison barracks maintaining, the sanctity of the caste-based eating and drinking norms was not possible. In the beginning, the number of prisoners was small and because of still smaller number of prisoners of a particular caste, the making of a distinct identity was not possible. Among the prisoners coming from the traditional Indian caste groups the desire to observe caste rules and prohibitions must have been there, but because of their small number and unfavourable circumstances, their full observance would not have been possible. It is mentioned that all the prisoners coming together in the same ship would call themselves *chalani bhai*, who would live amicably and without discrimination of high and low; clean and untouchable caste and would have eating-drinking relationship. On a closer look, we come to know that these prisoners must have tried to safeguard and observe some elements of their caste system according to circumstances.

Observance of caste rules has been related with respectability among the Indians.[3] The penal settlement officials were not allowed to do anything that would hurt caste feeling of the prisoners. Usually to the extent possible, British officials actually tended to raise caste feeling.[4] As the prisoners' number swelled, the basis for practising caste became stronger.

Anonymity also helped concealment of the caste identity. It is mentioned that two sweepers cheated people for many years by posing to belong to a high caste. One lived for many years as a Rajput (Rajvanshi) and the other served as a cook in a free Brahmin family posing as a Brahmin.[5] The contemporary events reveal a process of 'sanskritisation' among low castes. The low caste prisoners had a tendency to adopt such clothes and life-style, which they could not have done on returning to their villages on the mainland. There are also instances of conversion to Islam in order to raise one's social status. On the other hand, there are also instances where, even though not belonging to sweeper caste, people degraded their social status and posed as a sweeper in order to avoid hard life of coolie labour.[6]

In the early phase of colonisation, administrative officers tried to regulate matrimonial alliances and restriction was imposed on interreligious marriages. In 1881, the Hindus were divided into four broad categories on the 'varna' pattern. That is Brahmin, Kshatriya, Vaishya and Shudra and a rule was laid down that the prisoners could marry only in their own caste cluster. Although, the British officers used the caste divisions as a basis of governance yet it is also true that the transferred prisoners tried to the extent possible to maintain their caste behaviour. The Hindu customs differed indefinitely not only according to caste but place, too. In the then Port Blair, hardly any marriage would take place according to prescribed rituals.[7]

Among the local born of Port Blair, caste feelings existed but only in a limited way. It is interesting to find that those who are looked down upon as hybrid or cross-caste in India have been given social position in Port Blair society. The people had vague knowledge about their caste rites since the beginning.[8] Actually, descendants of the prisoners only know from which part of India their parents came. Their not understanding the actual nature of caste was but natural. Most prisoners would have come from patriarchal families and it is because of this that the local born knew only about their father's caste. It is mentioned that mother's caste was either unimportant or it was ignored. By starting this new tradition, they categorised caste in two broad divisions, that is, high and low. If we analyse it from the point of view of early caste history, the early settlers may be put only under high caste (*Savarna*) and low caste (*Avarna*). Children of Brahmin, Kshatriya and Vaishya belong to the former and Shudra and other low castes to the latter. It is only logical that continuance of the classical caste system was not possible in the given circumstances, but at the same time it did persist in terms of high and low castes.

In the context of role of caste in contemporary matrimonial alliances in Port Blair, it is mentioned that there were almost no cases of *anuloma* marriage. It was not possible to fully consider caste only as a result of contemporary circumstances. Yet, there was strong desire to marry only in one's caste and undoubtedly it was practiced to the extent possible.

Around 1911, caste system gradually began disintegrating. It is conjectured that "although in the prison system of Port Blair caste system of the prisoners has been accepted and after banishment several laws have also been framed to maintain it, yet after an interval, attack on monopoly of caste is inevitable".[9]

The British officers also kept in mind occupational basis of castes. Members of Brahmin and other upper castes would be given task of cook or other kitchen work and members of low castes, works like cleaning, etc. Kloss C. Boden writes: "Caste – a most important point in connection with people of India is carefully respected, and the Brahmin prisoners are nearly all employed as cooks."[10] But during early years of imprisonment the prisoners had to do physical labour together as labourers. Consequently occupational basis of caste was destroyed. There was no absolute freedom of choice of occupation. Whatever task was given had to be performed. The prison system arrangements were such that even though high caste prisoners were involved in kitchen or store, yet other tasks were so distributed, that they were compelled to have friendly relations and hang together with those with whom they would willingly have no contacts in the mainland.

Although the British officers, if they wanted, could take any work from the prisoners without consideration of the caste, actually they never did so. While taking work, caste prohibition was kept in mind. This is obvious from the letter[11] of the then Chief Commissioner to Government of India regarding contemplated decision to stop sending prisoner to penal settlement on banishment, warning about possible difficulty arising from death of low caste labourers especially sweepers and washerman, in free colony. He suggested that "...Government of India can, as they did in 1899, request local Governments to despatch so many term convict sweepers per year to Port Blair."

Dearth of sweepers would have naturally caused hygiene and sanitation problem in penal settlement. Because of non-availability of prisoners of a particular caste the Andaman administration could not take such work arbitrarily from a prisoner of some other caste which could offend his caste feeling. For this reason, government departments of mainland were consulted and requested to send prisoners of particular castes. It is mentioned that for want of members of sweeper community, Mopala prisoners were employed for cleaning the barracks and other places.[12] Once on account of shortage of sweepers in the colony, superintendent of Central Jail of Cannanore and Secretary to Madras Government had advised Chief Commissioner of the settlement that Mopala prisoners could be employed for cleaning.[13] The Superintendent, Central Jail, Cannanore wrote to Inspector General of Prisons, Madras, Ootacamund: "As the difficulty experienced at Port Blair for want of the sweeper class is probably also connected with the refilling of the settlements, with Mappilla deportees, I would mention that there is a fair proportion among them who could be put to barrack sanitation work. For the last 10 years or more, it has been the practice in this Jail to employ Mappillas as toties when other low caste prisoners were not available for the purpose... for if the Moppillas did not mind it in his own country he is not likely to object away from it."[14] But when this researcher desired corroboration from local Mopalas they denied it.

In the penal settlement, unity existed between Hindu and Muslims right since the beginning, but the Hindu maintained untouchability in matters of food and drinks. A Muslim could sit in a Hindu house but he could not eat or drink with the family, not even touch water or food. He was prohibited to enter their kitchen. The Hindus would distribute delicacies to

Muslims on their main festivals. Muslims too would distribute eatables among Hindus on their festivals but only in uncooked form. Similarly, in a community feast, staunch traditional Hindus would sit separately and there would be separate arrangement for their food. The high caste Hindus observed prohibitions about food and drink to the extent practicable. The low caste would be liberal regarding caste prohibitions.

Full observance of caste restriction on marriage was not possible because of dearth of women in the settlement since the very beginning. The total Hindu population was divided into two broad divisions: high caste and low caste and marriages would take place within these categories.

Some low caste Hindus embraced Islam or Christianity for personal gains or in the quest of high social status. But such converts were considered low by members of that religion. In the beginning, Protestant Christians were in majority and they considered themselves superior to the Catholics. But, gradually, the number of Catholics increased mostly because of conversion from low castes and tribals. Among the Christians, the Anglo-Indians were at the top. The Muslims with foreign lineage considered themselves superior to the converts. Converted Muslims and Christians laced their adopted religion with their local customs and caste culture. Although not apparently visible, right since the beginning, like the Hindus, a parallel caste system also existed in other religions.

Under new circumstances, many traditional caste occupations crumbled and thereby pulled down the very foundation of traditional hierarchical structure. The prisoners were exiled in individual capacity and not as family unit and lack of women particularly hindered reconstitution of a family, much less the traditional Indian joint family. Under these circumstances, caste assemblies and panchayats too could not thrive.

Generally, caste-based division and analysis of population is not done in census reports. Only once in the 1931 census, 512 low caste persons were counted. They were divided in this way: *Bhangi* 29, *Chamar* 204, *Kori* 47 and *Pasi* 232. Obviously, pretty large proportion of low castes was there in the early emigrant population.

During Japanese occupation, the caste system was so badly damaged that even later, during the period of social stability, it could not thrive. Low caste Hindus, by hiding their caste identity and not emphasising the norms of their caste behaviour followed the process of sanskritisation to some extent and refused to accept to belong to any low caste. In the 1951[15] and later census reports every one was listed under a special social category – 'non-backward caste'. No significance was given to recording caste membership in early emigrant society. But, the fact remains that there are many people of schedule caste origin in Andaman.[16] Most old timers know the caste origin of each other's family. But it is possible that in due course of time, because of the general practice of not using caste names, gradually people would not know about the other castes. Particularly among high caste families, disclosing their caste background even to neighbours and others may be done with some sense of pride. On this basis, it can be inferred that caste-consciousness is likely to be more common among those of high caste origin.

At present, a very loose form of caste system is to be found in Andaman. Caste prohibitions are observed according to convenience, or no particular significance is attached to them, although in villages there are still conservative families whose members would observe many rules of caste system as on mainland India. Only while establishing matrimonial alliance caste is considered, although marriage within caste is not considered essential. But normally a high caste person would not marry a low caste or tribal. A parallel caste system can be found among Muslims and Christians too and among them original followers consider the converts as low and generally do not favour marriage with them. Now, there is no question of social boycott or social or monetary punishment for transgressing caste rules. Generally, there is no naming of caste at all. Most people here do not have complete knowledge of their caste. Whatever idea or knowledge they have is vague and they have derived it by reading books, magazines or hearing from older people.

Because of the fact that there is no naming by caste and no great significance is attached to caste, many people say that early emigrant society of Andaman has no caste system at all. Such a conclusion is actually deceptive. Andaman society does have a caste system although its form has been modified according to circumstances and necessities of the society. People are aware of caste but its practice is quite loose. Still there are senior men and women who strictly observe their caste rules and norms. They fully observe untouchability in matters of food and drinks. There are also those who, if touched by Muslims or low castes, or on even coming under their shadow, would purify themselves by bath. It is a significant fact that in those families whose members have mixed blood from some other caste, or religion or cultural group, caste system is almost dead and they do not mention their caste at all, but the families that have maintained purity of blood (though very rare), do mention caste and to some extent, observe caste rules also. Senior members of most high caste families know who or which family belong to high caste or to low caste. The present generation of youth is generally not interested in caste. Functioning of caste system requires some bases. It is found that people migrating in large groups, and with people of similar cultural background, can recreate and maintain the caste system, in a given stratification pattern for that matter, but this is not feasible in any small emigrant group.

Determinants of Caste Status

In the understanding of the patterns of social stratification, differentiation between ascribed and achieved social status has been used as an important analytical tool. It is generally hypothesised that as traditional societies move towards modernisation, achieved status plays the more important part. There is increasing freedom of choice of professions. In the case of the Andamanese society, it was hypothesised that the change was rather arbitrarily imposed through administrative fiat. So, though caste attitudes may exist in muted form, it is at the same time true that caste really plays a very small part in determining one's status particularly economic/professional status.

In this place, there are developmental potentialities but all development avenues and resources are in government sector. Hence, the main source of livelihood is service. State administrative system has full command on the local economy. In a way, the islands may be called a controlled residential colony, with preponderance of works in public sector. The position in the administrative hierarchy plays the most important role in prescribing one's status. Only high government officials from early emigrant society may be included in this high class but as expected, one of the important qualities of an officer or administrator is to maintain a distance from others. It applies to this society also. It is worth mentioning here that merely sufficient income or money does not provide high position to a man. There are many instances where an individual has sufficient money but no corresponding social status. Generally, people in administrative service enjoy higher social status in comparison with others with same economic position. Most members of early emigrant community are in government service and they consciously try to maintain status. Bureaucratic culture also affects other spheres of society. Because of this also, the role of caste in prescribing social status becomes secondary, yet high caste origin and comparatively higher administrative post are definitely considered to be a hallmark of superior status.

Notes

1. Ghurye, G.S., "Caste and Race in India'" quoted by M.N. Srinivas in *Social Inequality*, 1968, p.269.
2. Ghurye, G.S., *Caste, Class and Occupation*, Popular Prakashan, Bombay, 1961, pp. 2-27.

3. *The Imperial Gazetteer of India*, Vol. XX, Oxford: The Clarendon Press, 1908, p.203.
4. Ibid.
5. Ibid.
6. Ibid.
7. Ibid., p.204.
8. Ibid., pp. 204-205.
9. *Census of India, 1911.*
10. Kloss, C. Boden, *Andamans and Nicobars*, Vivek Publishing House, New Delhi-7, 1971, p.27.
11. Letter from the C.C. of the Andaman and Nicobar Islands, No. 1112, dated 20 August, 1922 in Proceedings file No. 418, serial nos. 1-10, Home Department, Jails, N.A.I., New Delhi.
12. Letter from Superintendent, Central Jail Cannanore to Inspector General of Prisons, Madras, Octacamund, No.4156, dated 22 November, 1922 in the Proceedings file no. 418, serial nos. 1-10, 1922, Home Department, Jails, N.A.I., New Delhi.
13. Letter from R. Ramchandra Rao, Secretary to Madras Govt., Law (General Department), No.3168, dated 18 December, 1922 to C.C., A&N Islands, in the Proceedings file no.418. serial nos. 1-10, 1922, Home Department, Jails, N.A.I., New Delhi.
14. Letter No. 4156, dated 22 November, 1922, Proceeding File No. 418, Serial No. 1-10, 1922, Home Department, Jails, N.A.I., New Delhi.
15. *Census of India, 1951*, Vol. XVII, "Andaman and Nicobar Islands".
16. Letter to Editor "Light of Andamans'", *Weekly Newspaper, Port Blair*, Ramakant Haldar, "Scholarships for Students Studying in Mainland", November 3, 1980, p.2.

5 Marital and Family Life

We begin with a brief analysis of marital life in the earlier period with the help of information derived from secondary sources and then discuss institution of marriage and family at present, separately with the help of data collected from primary sources.

Marital and Family Life in Penal Settlement

The success of the plan to reform life-sentence prisoners banished to Andaman penal settlement was based on permission to prisoners to lead a family life during their sentence.[1] In the beginning of penal settlement itself, Indian government had accepted positive benefits of a stable family life.[2] For this it was essential to allow prisoners to bring their families from the mainland or to marry local women. The government gave full permission to prisoners of *gadar* (1857 rebellion) to bring their families from India. In 1858, 25 Bengalis expressed their desire to bring families from the mainland. But despite government efforts[3] the women and children refused to come to Andamans possibly because of imagined fear of dangerous and hard life of *Kala Pani* and apprehension that by crossing the sea they would be socially boycotted. During early years of penal settlement, probably, there was not a single woman in the colony. It is recorded that realising their importance the then superintendent had requested the Indian government to send some women.[4] In May 1860, the Bengal government was ordered by Government of India to send 30 women prisoners undergoing life-sentence, who were willing to go to Andaman. Colony superintendent was given permission to allow these women to marry or become 'self-supporter'.[5]

After undergoing a definite term of sentence when a prisoner reached the self-supporter status he was allowed to marry and settle in the island.[6] The prisoner who married a female prisoner was allowed to become a self-supporter. Soon many prisoners married. But shortly afterwards government had to put some restriction because it was found that the man with a short-sentence who married a life-sentence female prisoner, abandoned her after completion of his prison term. Therefore, the Indian government instructed Port Blair Superintendent to allow only those marriages where the married male prisoner has expressed the desire to settle down there, after completion of his sentence and becoming free.

Seeing the chances of proliferation of prisoners' descendants, prison officers had to discourage such marriages. But the immediate effect of this decision, according to Major Davis, was that about 400 marriageable women were desirous to marry quickly when permitted.[7] Though population data on female prisoners around 1867 is not available, yet it is necessary to mention here that the number of women waiting for permission to marry, i.e., four hundred was not small. At that time, the number of total female prisoners would have been only little more. The policy of restricting prisoners' marriages continued up to Captain Mann's time (1868-71). The bad result of such a policy was seen with increase in unnatural relationships among the prisoners. For want of adequate number of women, many women were married only for name's sake and were compelled into prostitution. The then Superintendent was desirous of imposing certain restrictions on marriage.[8]

Consequently, the government decided that only class I prisoners, who had become self-supporters, be allowed to marry.

The problem of marriage among prisoners became so complicated that in 1872 Campbell, who was deputed to inspect the colony, was also requested to study the issue of prisoners' marriage in Andaman.[9] On his recommendation, permission to marry was given to male prisoners after having attained class I (after a minimum stay of ten years) and to life-sentence female prisoners with two years' satisfactory conduct in class I category (after a minimum stay of five years). For the sake of prisoners' welfare and in the interest of morality, Sir Henry Norman was in favour of maximum marriages.[10] But he was against marriage between life-sentence prisoners and short-sentence prisoners. His recommendations were accepted by the government.[11] After implementing these rules, the government faced a new problem. A life-sentence prisoner was set free after completing 20 years of prison term and a male prisoner marrying after ten years had to reside in the colony for another ten years, whereas his wife who had permission to marry only after five years had to live there as prisoner for 15 years. Hence, after reconsidering the anomaly it was decided that permission for marriage should be given only when the Superintendent was satisfied "that the tie is one that would be binding on the parties under the personal law applicable to them in their own country" and that "the male convict should be clearly given to understand that he was contracting a permanent obligation".[12]

The Government of India also instructed the Superintendent, Port Blair to remit the unexpired period of sentence in the case of a well-behaved female convict whose husband was returning to India after release.[13]

Despite such liberal rules, problem of prisoners' marriage was not solved. Lyall and Lethbridge examined the possibility of increasing the number of female prisoners in the settlement. In their report, they clearly said that women were badly needed there as wives of self-supporters.[14] They realised that owing to the disproportionate sex ratio, sexual crimes and homosexuality was on the increase causing social and law and order problems. To help solve these problems they suggested that short-term sentenced female prisoners too, from Indian jails should be sent to Andaman. They felt that most convicted women were likely to settle down in Andaman after marriage. In due course, it was decided to transport such female term-convicts to Andaman who were sentenced for seven years or more. The Burmese prisoners were not included in it because of their meagre number.[15]

But this arrangement too did not have any significant effect. For the large number of male prisoners, the number of women remained insufficient. According to Andaman administration report on 31 March, 1897, the ratio between self-supporter males and females was 2447:363, i.e., seven men to every woman.[16] The dearth of women in the settlement led to moral degradation of prisoners. Unnatural sexual relationship and illicit relationship with women caused many crimes.[17] The situation deteriorated so badly that Superintendent Merck (1904-1906) said that immorality in the settlement was horrifying.[18] This vast imbalance could be easily understood by the available data on sex ratio of that time, that is 1874 to 1905-6.

Table 5.1

Sex Ratio in the Penal Settlement 1874 to 1905-6

Year	*Sex Ratio Among Criminals*	*Sex Ratio among Total Adult*
	Male:Female	*Male:Female*
1874	1:8.05	1:8
1881	1:9.16	1:8.85
1891	1:12.58	1:8.70
1901	1:15.36	1:8.96
1905-6	1:19.55	1:10.75

To do away with all legal impediments in the way, Widow Remarriage Regulation No. XV of 1856 was especially implemented in Andaman Nicobar isles.[19] It removed all legal impediments in way of a widow's remarriage. Regarding marriage of 'free' children of prisoners', Settlement Officer could advise guardians but he had no right to interfere in marriage customs and rituals of any section of 'free' population.[20]

District Officer had the right not to register any marriage between a girl below 10 and a boy below 12 years of age.[21] Data of 1901 census regarding the marriage of girls was as mentioned below:

Table 5.2
Marriage of Girls, 1901

Age	*Total Girls/ Women*	*Married*	*Unmarried*	*Widow*
Less than 5 years	182	2	180	–
5-10	126	11	115	–
10-15	123	38	82	3
15-20	101	79	15	7
Total	532 (100.0%)	130 (24.4%)	392 (73.7%)	10 (1.9%)

From the data in Table 5.2, it is difficult to say how 10 per cent of the girls below 10 years of age were married when the District Officer was empowered not to register such marriages. It is obvious from the data that mostly (60.8%) girls of 15 to 20 years of age were married. In the colony, 73.7 per cent of the girls of less than 20 years of age were unmarried which shows that during initial days practice of child marriage was not there.

In 1901, the marital status of the total population was as presented in Table 5.3.

Table 5.3
Marital Status, 1901

Marital Status	*Total Population*	*Male*	*Female*
Married	4,387 (26.9%)	3,762	625
Unmarried	10,458 (64.4%)	9,259	1,199
Widowed/Widow	1,411 (8.7%)	1,101	310
Total	16,256 (100.0%)	14,122	2,134

Marriage between prisoners and 'free' persons was prohibited but under special circumstances a self-supporter prisoner could marry a 'free' woman in Port Blair. Life-sentence male prisoner of class I, who was a self-supporter also, was allowed to marry or call his wife and children. Class I female prisoner with life-sentence or a definite period sentence was also allowed to marry locally.[22] Though self-supporter prisoners were allowed to call their families from mainland, they rarely did so or probably the family itself refused.[23] If marriage was according to social custom of the parties in a contract, with the permission of Colonial Officer, a self-supporter could marry a female prisoner. A Hindu could not marry a Muslim and un-divorced Muslim women with husband living in India too could not marry. The Superintendent would provide legal shape to marriage after registration.

So far as completing the marital rituals were concerned, it is to be mentioned that at that time there were many kinds of marriage rituals prevalent in India. In the penal settlement too, the concerned Colonial Officer would consent to the kind of marriage ritual the parties requested. The officers had no problem with Christian, Muslim, and Buddhist marriages because they had uniform marriage code and rituals but Hindu marriages would pose big problem because their customs and traditions varied with caste and place and this diversity made it impossible for marriage to fall in exact pattern. The 1909

Gazetteer mentions that hardly any marriage took place according to Hindu customs and traditions. In 1881, only four castes of Hindu were recognised in the colony, namely, Brahmin, Kshatriya, Vaishya and Shudra.[24] Hindu prisoners were intermarried. But before 1881 because of pressure of existing circumstances this marriage rule applied to marriage within the religion. Thus, it is clear that the Hindu prisoner was not able to observe three matrimonial prohibitions: endogamy, exogamy and *kuleen* (high-born) marriage. As mentioned earlier, as in Indian caste system developed fully among descendants of prisoners as in India, yet castes were reduced to two divisions: high caste and low caste. Children of *dvija* (Brahmin, Kshatriya, Vaishya) fathers were of high caste and the rest low caste. As far as possible, a male married the girl of his father's caste. Marriage within the caste was greatly desired and was performed also.[25] The caste system could not apply its full restrictions in the making of marriage.

All aspects of life in the colony were highly regulated. All decisions were subject to permission of British officers. Prescription and permission of marriage was vested in the administration. A certain amount of property was prescribed and he who wanted to marry must have possessed it.[26] Despite the policy of non-interference in marriage customs and traditions, rules of the administration indirectly affected the institution of marriage. The parties desirous of marriage had to fulfil certain formalities. Only application of fully eligible party was considered. Though the marriage-procession, *barat*, would go as per convention, yet prior permission was necessary and it could go only within limits of the village.[27] On one hand, government rules regulated the institution of marriage, on the other prevailing conditions in the colony were affecting it. Right from the beginning, there was lack of women and therefore, practices like prohibition of widow remarriage and problems like demand for dowry and divorce could not get established here. Control over child marriage up to certain age was there because of colonial rules. Rules of endogamy, exogamy and high born (*kuleen*) marriage could not become effective mainly because of relatively small number of women and ineffective reorganisation of caste system. This situation also had wide effect on prisoners' descendants during penal settlement period though the free descendants remained unaffected by different rules; yet in establishing relationship, owing to local conditions they even transgressed limits of caste and religion. For want of authentic facts, a detailed discussion on this aspect is not possible, yet it can be certainly said that a significant number of inter-caste and inter-religious marriages took place. Due to scarcity of women, traditional ideals of mainland Indian society regarding man-woman relationship broke down. Sexual morality declined. Many illegitimate children were born and many men kept more than one wife. Such situations also arose when, because of sexual relationship with many men, one woman gave birth to their children with different hereditary characteristics. Some women slept with British employees and gave birth to their children. People of different linguistic groups entered into marital relationship, which led to the necessity for a link language and mixed Hindi served this purpose widely. From the very beginning families were patriarchal. Usually, children stayed with their parents till they themselves got married. Tendency for establishing a separate house after marriage developed because of availability of plenty of vacant land. People could build houses easily on such land by cutting local forest. Besides, the government too would help and encourage house building.

During Japanese occupation many perished because of tyranny. Sensing the time of crisis prisoners' descendants united to face the situation. Socio-economic condition of the colony declined. Many inter-caste and inter-religious marriages took place during the period. Many Japanese soldiers had sexual relationship with local women with their consent, but there are instances of molestation too. Relationship with the Japanese resulted in illegitimate children.

After this brief analysis of family and marital life during early period of settlement, it is now proper to analyse separately the present state of family and marital life of emigrants on the basis of priorities.

Form of Marriage in Early Emigrant Society

Keeping in view the religion-wise population of early emigrants, the study is confined to Hindus, Muslims and Christians only. Although groups of tribal origin like Bhantu and Ranchi, are covered by Hindu and Christian divisions, yet keeping in view their nominal population in study area of Port Blair town, their marriage customs and rituals have not been included.

Hindu marriage is a sacrament whose aims are *dharma* (performance of religious duties), *praja* (progeny) and *rati* (sexual pleasure).[28] *Homa* (sacrificial fire), *panigrahan* (holding of bride's hand by the bridegroom) and *saptapadi* (seven steps around *homa*) are major acts without which the ritual is not complete. All these acts are performed under the direction of a Brahmin priest chanting Vedic *mantras* with the holy fire as witness. Among Hindus, there is no provision for annulment of marriage. Remarriage of widow is prohibited. Prohibition of endogamy and exogamy was also there in prevalence. Endogamy rule restricts marriage only within the caste or sub-caste. According to exogamy, marriage cannot take place in the same *gotra, pravar* and *pinda*. Traditionally, selection of the spouse rested with the parents.

Several factors have brought about wide ranging changes in the institution of marriage. Through many social legislations attempt has been made to reform the age-old anachronistic marriage customs like child-marriage, prohibition of widow's remarriage, restriction on inter-caste marriage, absence of right to divorce, dowry system, etc. Different Acts like Hindu Widow Remarriage Act 1856, Child Marriage Prohibition Act 1929, Hindu Women's Property Right Act 1932, Special Marriage Act 1872, 1923, 1954, Hindu Marriage and Marriage

Annulment Act 1955, Hindu Succession Act 1956, Hindu Minority and Custodian Act 1956, Dowry Prohibition Act 1961, etc. have widely affected the institution of marriage and family.

Muslim marriage, *nikah*, is a contract or social agreement which provides for *mahr* to the bride. The amount of *mahr* depends on the capacity of both the parties. The amount of *mahr* would be more for a virgin than that for a divorcee or a widow. Full amount of *mehar* is not paid in marriage and the custom varies from state to state regarding what part of the amount should be paid before consummation of marriage and what part after the hasband's death or annulment of the marriage. *Mehar* is paid only to that bride who was a 'free' woman.[29] A Muslim male could marry, in addition to a Muslim woman, a woman of any *al kitab* religion but a Muslim woman could not marry a non-Muslim. Islam allows four wives to a man and holds that men are superior to women. On Muslim marriage contracts signature of two witnesses, one from each party is essential, out of which one must be male. Islam also recognises marriage among cousins but it is prohibited between children of the same mother. Although divorce, *talaq*, is easy yet it is a one-sided right vested in the male only. The 1939 dissolution of Muslim Marriage Act has given divorce rights on different bases to women also. The educated class is increasingly going in favour of single wife.

According to Christianity, marriage is a very strong bond. Monogamy is considered ideal and it is commanded that every man will keep his wife and every woman her husband.[30] Second marriage is considered adultery. Mutual love between husband and wife is emphasised. Pre-marital sexual relationship is prohibited. According to Christianity, marriage is a sacrament whose social purpose is development of children, freedom from sexual tyranny, regular satisfaction of natural desires, building of family, etc. Concurrence of every member present in the church is necessary for Christian marriage. The priest performs marriage ceremony in presence of all. In Christian marriage, church membership certificate, certificate of good character, marriage application three weeks prior to marriage date is an essential condition. Christian society does not have child marriage, widow's remarriage and dowry problems. After brief analysis of marriage in three religions it seems necessary to mention that scholars like Merchant[31], Desai[32], Ghurye[33], Kapadia[34], Shah[35], Mathew[36], Cormack[37], Ross[38], Sharayu and Vanarase[39], Kanan[40], Mahajan[41], Fonseca[42], Hate[43], Kapoor[44], Mehta[45], and Mansingh Das[46], etc. have inferred that the old system of marriage is giving birth to a new system. In this context, it is but proper to analyse the present form of marriage institution of early emigrants on the basis of primary data.

Marital Status

In all, 147 families were chosen for sample study which consisted of 55.2 per cent Hindus, 41.4 per cent Muslims, 0.6 per cent Sikhs, and 2.8 per cent Christians. In total, there were 1,190 members in all families: 617 Hindus, 544 Muslims, 27 Christians, and 2 Sikhs. According to marital status of 617 Hindus, 36.9 per cent were married, 3.9 per cent widows, 1.5 per cent widowers, 0.2 per cent divorcees and the remaining 57.5 per cent unmarried. Similarly, out of 544 Muslim members, 36.8 per cent were married, 0.4 per cent widowers, 2.9 per cent widows, 0.2 per cent separated women, 0.7 per cent divorcees and the remaining 59 per cent unmarried. Among 27 Christians, 25.9 per cent were married, 3.7 per cent widowers, 6.4 per cent widows and the remaining 63 per cent unmarried. Since, there was only one Sikh family in the study, hence any analysis may be misleading. In the total, there are 0.1 per cent separated women, 0.4 per cent divorced men and women, 1.0 per cent widowers, 36.6 per cent married, and 58.3 per cent unmarried persons (see Table 5.4).

Table 5.4

Distribution According to Marital Status

	Married	*Widowers*	*Widow*	*Separated*	*Unmarried*	*Divorcee*	*Total*
Hindu	228 (36.9%)	9 (1.5%)	24 (3.9%)	-	355 (57.5%)	1 (0.2%)	617
Muslim	200 (36.8%)	2 (0.4%)	16 (2.9%)	1 (0.2%)	521 (59.0%)	4 (0.7%)	544
Sikh	-	-	1 (50.0%)	-	1 (50.0%)	-	2
Christian	7 (25.9%)	1 (3.7%)	2 (7.4%)	-	17 (63.0%)	-	27
Grand Total	435 (36.6%)	12 (1.0%)	43 (3.6%)	1 (0.1%)	694 (58.3%)	5 (0.4%)	1190 (100.0%)

Table 5.5

*Age-wise Distribution of Unmarried Female**

Religion	*Age (in years)*				*Total*
	Less than 16	*17-22*	*23-28*	*29 or above*	
Hindu	90 (60.4%)	44 (29.5%)	14 (9.4%)	1 (0.7%)	149
Muslim	114 (77.0%)	31 (21.0%)	–	3 (2.0%)	148
Christian	3 (42.8%)	2 (28.6%)	1	1 (14.3%)	7
Grand Total	207 (68.1%)	77 (25.3%)	15 (14.3%)	5 (1.7%)	304 (100%)

*Since, there was only one Sikh family in the sample hence it is not included.

If divided age-wise, most of the unmarried members were below the marriageable age or just of this age. Table 5.5 presents the description of unmarried female members age-wise. The table shows the proportion of unmarried among girls below 16 years of age: 60.4 per cent Hindu, 77.0 per cent Muslim, and 42.8 per cent Christian. In 17-22 age group, 29.5 per cent Hindu, 21.0 per cent Muslim, and 28.6 per cent Christian girls are unmarried. In 23-28 age group, 9.4 per cent Hindu and 14.3 per cent Christian girls are unmarried. In 29 and above age group, 0.7 per cent Hindu, 2 per cent Muslim and 14.3 per cent Christian women are unmarried. Certainly, this age group is much more than the desired marriageable age of girls.

If the figure for all unmarried girls in the sample is analysed age-wise, most (68.1%) are below marriageable age, 25.3 per cent are of marriageable age and 4.9 per cent are crossing this age. Yet, matrimonial alliances pose no problem. Only 1.7 per cent girls who have crossed marriageable age have some problem in this regard.

For the under 17-22 age group, the mean age of Hindu girls is 19.04 years, Muslims 18.9 years and Christian 19.5 years. In 23-28 age group, the mean age of Hindu girls is 25.2 years and of Christian girls 24.0 years. There was no Muslim girl from this age group. In 29 years and above age group, mean age of Hindu women was 37 years, of Muslims 31.6 years, and of Christian 33 years. This age group is obviously much above marriageable age. The Hindu girls of 23-28 years group could also be said to be crossing the marriageable age.

Table 5.6

Age-wise Distribution of Unmarried Males

Religion	*Age (in years)*				*Total*
	Less than 20	*21-25*	*26-31*	*32 or above*	
Hindu	148 (71.8%)	34 (16.5%)	14 (6.8%)	10 (4.9%)	206
Muslim	140 (80.9%)	27 (15.6%)	5 (2.9%)	1 (0.6%)	173
Sikh	1 (100.0%)	–	—	–	1
Christian	5 (50.0%)	2 (20.0%)	2 (20.0%)	1 (10.0%)	10
Grand Total	294 (75.4%)	63 (16.2%)	21 (5.4%)	12 (3.0%)	390 (100.0%)

Seen in totality, the mean age of 17-22 age group is 18.5 years, 23-28 group 25.2 years, and 29 and above group 33 years. We may conclude that only 6.6 per cent girls have crossed marriageable age, which may lead to their life-long unmarried state.

Unmarried male members of respondent families have also been analysed age-wise as shown in Table 5.6, which shows 71.8 per cent Hindus, 80.9 per cent Muslims, 100 per cent Sikhs, and 50 per cent Christians who are yet unmarried are of 20 years or below. In 21-25 age group, comes 16.5 Hindus, 15.6 per cent Muslims, and 20 per cent Christians. Under 26-31 age group, we find 6.8 per cent Hindus, 2.9 per cent Muslims and 20 per cent Christians are unmarried. Their mean age, 22.6 years is below marriageable age. Under 26-31 age group, there are 6.8 per cent Hindus, 2.9 per cent Muslims, 20.0 per cent Christians with mean age of 28.3 years. At present, they could be said to be of the right marriageable age. Only 4.9 per cent Hindus, 0.6 per cent Muslims, and 10 per cent Christians who are 32 years and above with mean age of 46 years which is much above the ideal marriageable age.

In brief, 5.5 per cent are in marriageable age and 3.1 per cent have passed marriageable age whose marriage seems improbable because in Hindus unmarried males of 32 years or above have mean age of 42.7 years, among Muslims 50 years, and among Christian it is 77 years.

There must be certain factors behind the circumstances of leading an unmarried life. Among unmarried females 1.6 per cent and among unmarried males 3.1 per cent are much above marriageable age. In the case of five women, an attempt was made to study the causes that might have led to the unmarried state. The profiles are given below:

Case Studies

1. Miss A (36 years) belongs to an ordinary Muslim family and works as a clerk. Her father also worked as a scribe. The financial condition of the family was bad in the beginning so her father could not get her married. Meanwhile her mother died. Father's work stopped because of bad health. Under these circumstance, it

became impossible for the family to make both ends meet. Being the eldest in the family she had to work as a clerk. Full liability of the family fell on her shoulders. She felt it her duty to educate her younger brother and sister. The problem as to who would look after the family after her marriage stopped her from marrying. She got her sister married to a ward attendant. The brother was not taking interest in studies, which he left and picked up a job and soon after he too got married. By now Miss A was too old to find a match for herself and did not find it proper to marry at such a late age. At present, her sister's and brother's family live with her. The brother earns Rs 250, the sister's husband Rs 350 and she herself earns Rs 550 per month. She still controls family finance.

2. Miss B (33 years) a Christian nurse is educated up to class XI. People of her community doubted her character. She had gone to mainland India for nursing training and had illicit relationship with some persons, which came to be known to some people in her community. After she returned from training her family tried to marry her but could not because of her ill-repute.
3. Miss C (26 years) is a high school pass Muslim woman and works as a clerk. Her father was a Malabari Nayar and her mother a Mopala Muslim. When she was just of two years, her father was sentenced for murder. Her mother handing her over to her sister married another person. On release from jail, her father set up some business on Diglipur island and sent her for nursing training to mainland India where she fell in love with a doctor who was willing to marry her but suddenly came a telegram asking her to come immediately since father had a paralytic attack. She immediately left to take care of him and thus her training was discontinued. Then she tried for a job. During this time, she fell in love with a local Madrasi boy, who promised to marry but ditched her. This relationship brought her ill repute. Shortly, thereafter she began to live

with her paternal aunt (*phuphi*) who was involved in flesh trade. Although *phuphi* did not enter her in the trade yet living with her brought further disrepute. Then she again had an affair with a local Madrasi boy who also promised to marry. At present, she has such a bad name that there are no chances of marriage.

4. Miss D (45 years) a Hindu nurse had to carry the liability of mother and brothers because of father's death. Her brother was studying medicine and she wanted him to continue to become a doctor and she did not marry until he completed his education. Later because of age the offers that came demanded much dowry. Hence, she could not get married.
5. Miss E (37 years) a Hindu, educated up to class IX, stays at home. In her family, there are her parents, five brothers, three sisters and wife of a brother. Her elder brother got married at the age of 38. She was pretty and her parents wanted a suitable match and refused many local offers. Time passed and because of her little education she could not find a job. Later, her parents were ready to accept even the most ordinary offer but because of her age it could not be done.

The above case studies indicate specific factors for the subjects not getting married. Actually, local girls want to marry professionals of high standing like doctors and engineers and search for such alliances takes a lot of time leading to a situation where because of advanced age even finding an ordinary match becomes difficult. And if an offer is available, dowry demand is so high that marriage is not possible. Besides, bad reputation is another factor. Sometimes it is family the liabilities. A significant observation is that at present the tendency to marry an earning girl is on the increase. Earlier, marrying working girls was not considered proper, but later when new emigrant Malayali girls went in for jobs, early emigrant girls also followed them. At present, non-working girl's marriage is a problem.

Let us now study factors behind male unmarried status through the following case studies:

1. Mr A (38 years), a Muslim is employed and comes from a well-off family. In youth he fell in love with a Muslim girl whose family was conservative and refused permission for marriage because the boy drank too much. Frustrated in love he decided not to marry at all.
2. Mr B (52 years), a Hindu is invalid and because of that remained uneducated. Hence, he could not be married. Another family member of 47 years is also unmarried. One family member suffered form T.B. and it became known in the small place, where none wanted to marry into a diseased family. However, some members of the family had love marriage.
3. Mr C (46 years), a Hindu is the son of a high official of Andaman forest department. He is educated up to class IX and helps his elder brother in business who is actually responsible for being an obstacle to his marriage. The elder brother was in possession of property and commanded full regard from his younger one. However, he (elder brother) did not bother about his (the younger one) marriage when he attained the marriageable age. He was dejected and spoke to his *bhabhi* (brother's wife). Without actually making any effort to find a match, the brother said that he was trying for a suitable match. Mr C's friends took him to some local women of loose character for sexual gratification. After quite some time of such indulgence, Mr C felt that his potency had declined. Once, when he asked a prostitute if he was able to satisfy her, she replied in negative, which led him to believe that what he thought was true. Yet he was not worried. After taking different medicines for some time he went again for copulation and felt that he had premature ejaculation. He felt very bad and thought why to marry and spoil a girl's life. So he decided to remain unmarried for good.

Thus, the reasons for the males remaining unmarried are physical disability and failure to marry a girl of choice.

Selection of Spouse and Role of Mediator

When the boy comes of age and stands on his own legs parents ask friends, relatives, and concerned religious priests to inform about suitable girl. They work as mediator for matrimonial alliance between two families. Efforts are made for marriage between families of same status. The boy's parents or guardian after inquiring about the girl's character, education, employment, family condition, etc., send the mediator to the girl's houses with proposal. The girl's family too make full inquiry about the boy's family members, their nature and behaviour, his habits, character and personality, etc. Both the parents also inquire if there is any hereditary defect or disease in the family. When the girls party is satisfied with the details then they ask the mediator for an offer. It is not necessary that the offer should come from the girl's side or the boy's. Either party may do so. Usually, there is no question of rejecting the girl after seeing her because everything is already settled. Among the Hindus to complete the formality of choosing the girl, a ritual is performed and the boy's party gift her a ring, saree and other things according to their capacity. This formality is called *gode bharai* (filling the lap). The boy's guardian also invites the girls' party to see the boy. But mostly they do not go. If they see the boy, they have to give him something.

Among the Christians, when both parties are agreed, they have to inform the concerned church three weeks earlier. Among the Muslims too boy's proposal is taken to girl's family by some senior mediator. When the girl's party after thorough enquiry is satisfied, they give acceptance through the mediator. Some seniors of the boy's family go to the girl's and settle *nikah* which is called *mangani* (engagement). On the same day marriage date and *mehar* amount is also fixed, along with size of marriage-party and number of person's of girl's family going to the boy's house after marriage – *vidai*. The amount of money to be given to the boy as *tilak* (called *keting gijje* by Malayali-speaking Muslims) is also fixed.

Every effort is made to have matrimonial alliance in same religion. In family settled marriage special attention is paid on religion, caste (high or low), sect (e.g., Roman Catholic or Protestant among Christians and Shia or Sunni among Muslims). If the boy or girl goes in for love marriage family folks and relatives advise to marry in same religion. Girl's guardians are more rigid in this than of boy. The party socially and economically superior is wooed and persuaded. But stubborn boy or girl may compel parents to concede, in which case marriage is performed by family folks otherwise boy and girl elope and marry. Such elopers generally have good relation with mother, but not with father. In this case of inter-religious marriages if one of the parties agree, then the marriage is performed according to the religion or community of that party. When both the parties refuse either lovers elope and marry, or drop the idea. There are many instances of parent's refusal for marriage within or outside the religion. Usually such families are conservative. We can find Hindu-Muslim, Muslim-Christian, Bhantu-Mopala, Bhantu Hindu-Muslim, Bhantu Christian-Christian marriage here which are inter-religious, inter-caste, and inter-group.

Love marriages have social recognition. Marriage either settled by family, or by boy and girl has equal standing. However, parent fixed marriage within the same community and religion is considered more desirable.

Among Hindus, besides religion, caste is also a factor to some extent. Though no clear caste structure is to be found yet high caste Hindus do not marry among schedule caste and tribes. Older people know who belongs to schedule caste or tribe. That is why in marriage proposals social position of the entire family is definitely looked into. Marriage between high castes does not entail any severe restriction, yet Brahmins generally avoid to move out of their caste.

In the course of data collection, we came to know that 99 per cent boys and girls know each other before marriage. Mostly guardians ask the boy to inform his own choice of a girl of good character and education. Special consideration is given to girl's choice also, except in conservative families. A significant fact is that the boy or girl falls in love within their own religiôn and try to marry. Girls are considered family 'honour', hence there is more family control over them.

Case Studies

Through following case studies, we have tried to describe obstacles put by the family in the way of love marriage:

1. Mr A, a Hindu fell in love with a Muslim girl. His father did not like her intimate relationship with a Muslim girl. Mr A wanted to marry her but his father declined outright. When he stuck to it, the father agreed but Mr A had to leave his house. Mr A worked in the forest department. After marrying her, he lived in a rented house in Haddo. His wife abandoned Islam, embraced Hinduism and started living like a Hindu woman wearing *saree*, *sindoor* in hairparting, and *tika*. Mr A left his house because of his father but his other family members would sometime come to see him without the knowledge of his father. When his wife was in family way, his mother, brother and sister would come to look after her and stayed there, which caused trouble in the family. They put great pressure on the father to take him back. First, he did not agree but on great entreaty he said, "Do whatever you want. I won't say a word." Immediately, they brought home Mr A, his wife and baby. Now, Mr A's father is reconciled.

In love marriages, religious conversion too has a vital role. If one party converts according to the other, it has great influence on his/her acceptance by the family. The following example would suffice:

2. A Pandey Brahmin boy married a Muslim girl against his family's wish. Naturally, the conservative Brahmin family kicked him out. The boy, a lab assistant, lived separately with his wife. A son was born but even after many years,

his parents did not accept Mr Pandey, the main reason being that his wife refused religion-conversion.

3. The unmarried, unemployed 35 years old Roman Catholic, Mr C's love story is very moving. Ten years ago, he was a lab assistant in fishery department when he fell in love with a pretty Muslim girl living opposite his house. Love bloomed and he would stealthily slip into her room. They indulged in sex every day. When his family members come to know of it, they tried to dissuade him but he stuck to his desire to marry her. His elder brother hung him upside down (his father was dead), gave the fume of chilli and belaboured him. Mr C gave up food. His mother would somehow feed him. In frustration, he quit his job and went for six-month training to Madras. Meanwhile, the girl was married to a Muslim driver. After sometime, he abandoned her on charge of adultery and then divorced her. After 6-7 months Mr C returned. Once again, he resumed love with the divorced girl. This time, his mother, brothers and other relatives badly beat him with iron rod and sent him to police station. Two days later, after release, he came home with bowed head. He felt so humiliated that he left for Madras. Two months later, he returned with long hair and beard. Since, then he neither worked nor married, or cut his hair. He lives like this on income from house rent.

When parents do not agree for love marriage and the girl becomes pregnant, the family gets her married according to their religious customs to save face. When the boy's family comes to know of it, they also get the boy married according to their own religious customs. The following case is an example:

4. Telagu-speaking Hindu, Mr D is a junior clerk whose father is a male nurse. Mr D is married to an Anglo-Indian girl. Their affair continued for eight years but both families were against marriage. The boy's family declined on religious ground and the girl's family because boy's family was economically more inferior. But the lovers had

sworn to marry. Whenever the girl's parents talked of marriage she said that she would marry only after doing B.A. But when they came to know of the affair, they fixed her marriage with an army Major. The girl went to him and told him of her love affair. He withdrew himself. Meanwhile, the girl became pregnant. When her parents came to know of it, they got her married with Mr D in a church to save face. When Mr D's father came to know, they were married once again in a temple. The girl embraced Hinduism. Now, she is living happily with her husband and his parents.

Premarital sex and pregnancy may force parents, howsoever, adamant against marriage to fall in line in order to save 'family honour', lest it is dragged into any scandal, as is exemplified from the following case:

5. Mr E, nephew of an Executive Engineer, fell in love with a pretty well-built Bangala Deshi girl. In due course, she became pregnant. When abortion could not materialise, the girl asked for marriage for which neither the boy nor his family was ready. But, when the girl threatened to go to the police, the boy's family agreed in order to save its honour and she delivered just three days after marriage.

Freedom of Individual Choice

In family-settled marriage, consideration is given to boy's and girl's choice. Not that parents fix marriage on their own. Both boy and girl are consulted about the proposal. Marriage is not fixed by force. When guardians like a girl but the boy does not, all efforts are made to convince or change his mind. If girl rejects the boy, her wish is also given importance.

The opinion of 174 respondents was asked on personal like of the boy and girl in family-settled marriage and all said that there should be freedom of choice. However, some Muslim respondents opined that if family approves of boy there is no question of girl's choice.

Dowry

In India, dowry is a great obstacle in marriage. In context of early emigrant society, it is not yet a problem, but gradually it is becoming a problem. As a result of the preference to marry an earning girl, if the girl is not earning anything at the time of marriage the groom's family demands a fixed amount of money or some costly items, like ornaments of fixed value, scooter, sofa, house, plot of land or electronic goods, etc. Generally, well-off people take pride in giving sufficient dowry to their daughters and try to marry their sons and daughters in families of equal status. Girls of bad repute as well as uneducated and unemployed girls may remain unmarried for lack of dowry. Here is an instance. Mr. A, a doctor, is married to a pretty Hindu girl who was for many years having an affair with a local Pathan Muslim man. Her loose character was known to all yet Mr. A married her because she brought dowry of Rs 40,000 in cash. But there are also instances where the groom's family demanded dowry, but he even left his house in order to marry the girl without dowry. There is also a tendency to look for a rich girl who may bring maximum money or material. In Muslims no special demand is made as to the amount of *mehar* and *tilak* but it is a mere formality. However, even among Muslims and Christians, marriages are fixed after having a prior estimate of things to be given in marriage.

Fixing Marriage Date

When both the parties agree, the date of marriage is fixed mostly during vacations or holidays like second Saturdays, Sundays or some other holiday.

Among Muslims, boy's family members go to the girl's house to see her, follow the formality of *mangani* and gift her a ring, etc. Then another meeting is held for fixing the marriage date. On the fixed day, seniors of the boy's family and close relatives go to the girl's house with *mullah* (priest) who suggests a date keeping in mind planetary position and *nikah* date and other things are fixed. The girl receives gifts of clothes and ornaments. Marriage cannot take place during period of Muharram.

Among Hindus, when alliance is fixed the priest is asked to suggest an auspicious date and after studying the boy's and the girl's horoscope he suggests the date. The locals say that comparing of horoscope is in the priest's hand. If the date is convenient to both parties it is fixed or some other convenient date is fixed. Among Hindus, it is not necessary that marriage date must fall on a holiday.

Among Christians, after agreement of both parties they go to their respective church, Roman Catholic or Protestant, and apply to the priest three weeks before marriage, who after declaring the date, usually a Sunday, invites objection to the proposed alliance, and in the absence of any, the marriage takes place in the church.

Marital Age

Child marriages as such are not found although marriage of girls below 18 may be traced. However, it is significant that there is hardly any case of marriage where the boy is below 20-21 years mainly because a boy's marriage takes place only after he is fully self-dependent.

There is no fixed rule as to how much younger the bride should be to the boy. But a gap of 3-4 years is considered good. Unmatched marriages are not seen.

To the question about the proper age of boy's marriage, majority of the respondents (72.4%) answered 21-25 years. Religion-wise, 7.3 per cent Hindus opined 16-20 years, 19.8 per cent 26-30 years and the rest (72.9%) 21-25 years. The Muslim respondents fall in this break-up: 19.4 per cent 16-20 years, 8.3 per cent 26-30 years, and 72.3 per cent 21-25 years. Among Christians 20 per cent said 16-20 years, 20 per cent 26-30 years and remaining 60 per cent 21-25 years (see Table 5.7).

We have also tried to calculate the average age of marriage for boys, which comes to 24.06 years. Religion-wise the analysis shows that according to the Hindus the average age for the marriage of boys is 24.6 years, for the Muslims it is 23.2 years, for the Sikhs it is 25 years and for the Christians it is 24.2 years.

Table 5.7
Distribution of the Respondents According to the Proper Age of Marriage for Boys

Religion/Age	*16-20*	*21-25*	*26-30*	*Total*
Hindus	7 (7.3)	70 (72.9)	19 (19.8)	96 (56.8)
Muslims	14 (19.4)	52 (72.3)	6 (8.3)	72 (40.0)
Sikhs	–	1 (100.0)	–	1 (0.5)
Christians	1 (20.0)	3 (60.0)	1 (20.0)	5 (2.7)
Total	22 (12.6)	126 (72.4)	26 (14.9)	174 (100.0)

Note: Figures in parentheses denote percentage.

Further, to the question about the proper age of girl's marriage the majority (69.5%) of the respondents answered 16 to 20 years. Religion-wise, 6.3 per cent of Hindus opined 15 years or less than that, 63.5 per cent respondents 16 to 20 years and the rest 30.2 per cent 21 to 25 years. The Hindu respondents fall in the track up: 6.9 per cent 15 years or less, 77.8 per cent 16 to 20 years, 13.9 per cent 21 to 25 years and 1.4 per cent 26 years or more. According to the Sikh respondents, it should be 16 to 20 years. Among Christians, 60 per cent said about 16 to 20 years and the rest (40%) said that it should be 21 to 25 years. The suggested average age (religion-wise) of marriage for girls comes to 18.9 years.

On comparison between the respondents' real age at the marriage and suggested 'ideal' age, among Hindus the difference was merely 0.6 year. Among Hindus and Muslims, we find a downward tendency regarding boy's proper marriageable age because the average age of the respondents at the time of marriage was 24.8, whereas their considered proper marriageable age for boys is 23.2 years. Among Christians, we find an upward tendency. Their average age at their time of marriage was 24 years whereas their considered age is 24.4 years. On the whole too, we find downward tendency regarding actual age at marriage and suggested marriageable age, i.e., the figures being 25 years actual and 24.06 years suggested age.

Similarly, if we analyse girls' marriageable age on the same criteria as above following facts come up. The Hindu respondents consider 19.4 years as proper age whereas their wives were 18.5 years at the time of marriage. Here, we find an upward tendency. Average age of the Muslim respondent's wives at the time of marriage was 20.2 and suggested age is 18.2 years. Here, we find downward tendency. Among Christian respondents, we find upward tendency with average age of wives at the time of marriage being 16.5 and suggested age 20 years.

As compared with the respondents' own age at marriage, on the whole, we find a downward trend regarding 'ideal' marriageable age for girls, the suggested norm works out to 18.9 years (see Table 5.8).

Table 5.8

*Respondents and Their Wives' Age at Marriage**

	Hindu	*Muslim*	*Christian*	*Total*
Average Age at the Time of Marriage	25.2	24.8	24.0	25.0
Average Age of Marriage of Wives	18.5	20.2	16.5	19.2
Average Age Difference between Respondents and their Wives	6.7	4.6	7.5	5.8

* Since, there was only one Sikh respondent, therefore, it was found not proper to give his data.

The actual causes for the downward trend in 'ideal' marriageable age of boys and girls cannot be explained. At the same time, it is true that the struggle for survival on the island has certainly eased and life has become leisurely. So, the respondent might like to go for early marriage.

Preparation for Marriage

After the date is fixed, marriage preparations begin. The house is cleaned and if possible white washed. Neighbouring land is cleaned and the house is decorated with coloured paper flags. Small electric bulbs are used. Leaves of *madi* shrub are used as festoon, *madawa* and decoration. Since Christian marriage is performed in the church so those capable of it decorate the church. The families performing marriage in the cultural centre decorate it.

A day before the marriage, there is much activity and life in the houses of both parties with the arrival of relatives and friends who are sent invitation for the occasion. However, guardians of bride and bridegroom are given invitation in person as it is considered proper.

Before departure of *barat*, the marriage party and guests are treated with delicacies. Reaching the bride's house, they are again fed. Most local Hindus offer *puri, kheer, biryani,* etc.

Preparation at Bride's House

After fixing of marriage date, preparations begin at the bride's house. Marriage gifts and other items are purchased.

Among Hindus and Muslims on marriage day *madawa* or *mandap* is erected. The whole house and nearby land is cleaned. The house is decorated with *madi* leaves, colourful flags, and electric bulbs. Usually, South Indian marriage is performed during daytime. For want of space marriages are also performed on open ground of cultural centres. The feast expense is borne by both parties among the Christians. At times, some other place is chosen for feast and arrangement is looked after by the family members.

Since Christian marriages are performed in the church they do not have to arrange the priest who is already informed. Both parties reach the church on the fixed date and time. The priest to perform marriage among Hindus is to be arranged by bride's party. Similarly, among Muslims they have to invite a *mullah* to perform *nikah*.

Among the Hindus the bride's family goes to the bridegroom's house with *tilak* on the day of marriage, which contains gifts, dry fruits, fresh fruits and flowers. Thereafter, the ceremony is performed by the priest. Bride's party returns during day or in the evening. The turmeric given by the bride-groom party is applied to the bride and then she is bathed. This ritual is not observed by Muslims and Christians. Before the arrival of *barat* the bride is beautified by close relatives and friends. There is no special rule as to which particular relative will drape her saree and beautify her.

Marriage Procession (*Barat*)

Marriage is an occasion for celebration. Music and dance clearly indicate the gaiety of the occasion. Usually, there are no band parties accompanying, since there are no such groups here. Sometimes police or military band may be seen in attendance. *Barats* go by bus, car, truck, scooter or motorcycle. Band is replaced by playing of records on loudspeakers. Firework is used and boys dance at the head of *barat*.

Women, girls and children also go in *barat*. The bride-groom sits in a decorated car with close relatives, led by boys on scooters and motorcycles and followed by other members in buses, trucks, etc. Since Christian marriages are performed in the church, both bride and bridegroom go there in decorated cars along with other members. The bridegroom's party reaches first and then the bride's. Expenses on the *barat* may be borne by either of the parties.

Among Muslims, as in mainland India, when the *barat* departs, parents give their blessing in popular belief that they have same sweet relation with him after he is married. *Mullah* wishes for the success of marriage and sweets are distributed to all. Among Hindus, at the time of departure of *barat*, gods and goddess are remembered and among Christians, people pray before Christ's and other apostles' images. In Hindu and Christian *barat*s parents also go, but not among the Muslims. In some places, the brides or bridegroom's family present song and *kawwali* at the marriage venue.

Marriage Ceremony

Several rituals are performed between arrival and departure of *barat* which vary in different religions. Hence, they are described separately.

When a Muslim *barat* reaches the bride's house, her younger brother carries the bridegroom in his lap to *madawa,* although it is not a necessary custom. At the entrance to *madawa,* the bride's younger brother stands with a kettle of water, which is sprinkled on the bridegroom's feet. His feet are washed by bride's brother, for which he is given gifts in cash or kind, but there is nothing prescribed. It depends on one's pleasure and capacity.

Before performance of *nikah* the priest tells the bride that her marriage is fixed to so and so and so much is the *mehar* amount. He asks if she agrees and when she replies in affirmative or to keep mum it is taken as acceptance and then *mullah* performs *nikah* after reading ayats of the Koran and Fatia. After reading the *nikah, mullah* gives the bride's father's hand in the bridegroom's. Then the bridegroom says, "I accept your daughter". Then, the *mullah* enters in the mosque marriage register names of the bide, the bridegroom, their fathers, and marriage date and puts his signature along with signatures of two responsible senior persons as witness. Then people eat. After that the people leave, except some seniors of bridegroom's party, bridegroom's sisters and their friends who take the bride, her parents and close relatives to the bridegroom's house. All this happens on the nikah night. Women welcome them at the bridegroom's house-door and the bridegroom's sister washes the bride's feet. Then the couple is taken inside. All are offered *sharbat* (a sweet cold drink) and singing and dancing takes place. Then, people eat and the bride's parents take leave handing over their daughter to the bridegroom's parents. The *nikah* of widow or divorcee is plain and simple with only *nikah* ceremony, and none other.

Among Christians, on the fixed time and date both parties reach the Church, first the bridegroom's then the bride's. The bridegroom's party welcomes the bride's party. Church priest performs engagement and marriage ceremony. Both are told about matrimonial alliance and the priest administers the oath. Then, they shake hands and exchange rings. The priest asks bride's parents formally to gift the bride and declaring the 'holy alliance' reads from the Bible. It is to be noted that the priest can perform three or four marriages simultaneously at one place and time. In the church office, in presence of priest, the marriage document is filled up and as proof of marriage bride and bridegroom put their signatures to it. The priest offers tea to the couple and explains to them the Christian view on marriage. Significantly, he also tells them about the religion's prohibition of birth control.

Then, both parties go to the place fixed for a feast. Expenses on wedding feast are borne equally by both the parties. After the feast, bride's parents hand her over to the bridegroom. Sometimes a child from the bride's family accompanies them. Now-a-days bride's parents also go to the bridegroom's house. At the bridegroom's house the couple is received by women and taken inside.

Different rituals are performed among Hindus, but marriage ceremony does not take much time. The *barat* is received at bride's house by seniors of bride's party. Then, bride's mother performs *arati* of the bridegroom. She carries a *thal* with seven lighted lamps and after performing *arati*, she throws away the lamps in seven different directions. Then, the bride's younger brother carries the bridegroom in his lap to the *mandap* where the couple is seated and marriage ritual is performed by the priest. After going around the sacred fire seven times (saptapadi), the bride and bridegroom garland each other. Then people eat. Thereafter, bride's party goes to bridegroom's house with his party. There, bridegroom's mother or other family women perform *arati*. A round heap of rice husk, symbolic of hill of adversities, is put at the doorstep, which is kicked away by the bride. Then the couple is seated inside. Here feasting takes place. Then in the night, handing over the bride to the bridegroom, the bride's parents leave along with their party.

On wedding day, the bride receives gifts and cash from parents, relatives, and friends which is her personal property and she takes it to her husband's house.

First Coming of Bride to Her Parents' House After Marriage

Among Hindus, Muslims and Christians this visit is called *Chauthi,* which is a day of celebration. Although the word means fourth day, it is not necessarily observed on that day. Generally the bride comes to her parent's house six days after marriage. Since most marriages take place on holidays, so this is also fixed on a holiday.

Among Christians, the bride's parents or guardian go to the groom's house. Among Hindus, the parents do not go but some senior member goes. Among Muslims, children and bride's close relatives go. Having lunch there, they come home with the bride, groom and his family members and friends. As the bridegroom comes for the first time after marriage, so he is given special attention. Delicacies are offered. Bride's family folk indulge in pranks and jesting, teasing the groom like adding salt to *sharbat*, putting *neem* leaves in vegetable, or putting *papad* under the seat, etc. The food offered on this occasion is considered auspicious. Therefore, it is to be had even if it is not tasty with some inedible material. Refusing food is considered bad and people make fun of it. The groom may just taste and than leave it. On the next day after lunch, the bride goes away with the bridegroom and his party to her in-laws. Thereafter, she may come to her parental house any time but then no celebration takes place.

Divorce

Divorces do take place, though it is not easy and common. When marital discord becomes grave and no solution is found, then only divorce is resorted to. Man or woman, or both may initiate the proceedings. Since remarriage is socially accepted, divorced men or women face no problem. Yet, the innocent party is viewed sympathetically.

Divorce is rare among Hindus. Among Christians, there is no such provision. Yet, separation may be seen which is nominal. The main cause of separation is adultery by one of the parties. Comparatively, divorce is frequent among Muslims, more so among Mopala Muslims.

Respondents were asked whether divorce should be allowed or not. On the whole, only 22.4 per cent favoured and most, 77.6 per cent, were against it. Though the majority went against it, they felt that, if the problem is grave and insoluble, in that case the innocent party might seek divorce. Divorce on petty matters must not be allowed.

The respondents favoured equal rights to men and women as regards divorce. Nearly 12.5 per cent Hindus felt the right should be given to both the parties, 20 per cent Christians, and 34.7 per cent Muslims also thought so. All Sikhs also agreed.

Grounds for Divorce

Respondents were also asked to give their opinion about grounds for divorce. The usual grounds are religious conversion, insanity, adultery, gambling and drinking, leprosy or other contagious disease, etc. The respondents have mentioned more than one factor. Hindu, Muslim, Sikhs and Christian all consider adultery as the main ground. Among Hindus, 41.7 per cent consider mutual difference, 33.4 per cent woman's lunacy and 16.7 per cent woman's sterility as ground for divorce. Among Muslims, the response pattern is: 60 per cent for lunacy, 36 per cent for sterility. However, women's grounds for divorce are somewhat different. Around 66.7 per cent Hindus consider man's adultery as ground for divorce whereas among Muslims it is 48 per cent. All Sikhs and Christian respondents have considered it as a ground. In all 41 per cent Hindus and 36 per cent Muslims and all Sikh and Christian respondents have considered husband's indulgence in gambling and drinking as a ground. If a husband beats his wife, in that case 33.4 per cent Hindus, 40 per cent Muslim and all Christian respondents consider it as a fit ground for divorce.

Case Studies

Besides the grounds given by the respondents, we find some other grounds too, as revealed by the following two case studies:

(1) Mr A has married a second time. Describing himself a conservative in religious matters, he had his marriage (*nikah*) in 1952. Exactly six years later, he took divorce on the ground that his wife interfered in his religious observances. "Everyday at the time of *namaz*, my wife would come to me and ridicule me. She did not like my reading *namaz*, considered it useless and mocked at me. Many times, I tried to explain to her but all in vain. Looking at her activities, I prepared a talisman and gave her to wear it. Through it, I had prayed to God to give her good counsel. Smelling something suspicious, she showed it to her parents who gave it to *mullah* to find out if there was anything wrong. When I realised that my wife and in-laws were looking at me with suspicion, I felt mad and went to Jama Masjid (of Port Blair) *mullah* and gave him affidavit for divorce. The mullah conceded that the talisman was for the well being of the wife. He too blamed the wife and in-laws. *Mullah* decided in favour of my affidavit and divorce was granted."

Among Muslims, women have no right to divorce. If she wants to do so it is done through someone. A Muslim woman can divorce her husband on ground of impotency.

(2) Mrs A, a Muslim is married to a Muslim. She is quite pretty with full body, much superior to her husband.

Because of the husband's premature ejaculation, she would not be satisfied and with the help of her parents she applied to the *mullah* for divorce and told him the reason. On this ground, she was granted divorce.

Sometimes, it is found that a girl has to work too much in her in-laws house and she has no freedom, so she asks her husband to live separately and if he does not, differences crop up and when it reaches the breaking point, it leads to divorce. Sometimes, a girl is too attached to her parents and wants her husband to live with her at her parent's house. But if the husband is not prepared and the girl is stubborn, a situation for divorce is created. After divorce, children mostly live with mother as also children of abandoned wife.

Remarriage of Divorced Women and Widows

Second marriage of widows, divorcees, widowers and desertees is common. But, among Christians, divorcees and desertees are not allowed to remarry and it is rare. It is frequent among Muslims. Hindus do not consider widow's marriage good, although such marriages do take place. There are no rigid rules. Rules are flexible. Young widows can marry. Similarly, innocent party in divorce gets sympathy from the society.

Awareness About Divorce and Remarriage Rules

Though remarriage of widows, widowers, divorcees, and desertees has social recognition, there is little awareness about concerned government acts. Most of the respondents are acquainted with their respective religious rules.

Asked about these enactments, 96.6 per cent of the respondents showed their ignorance. Only 4.2 per cent Hindus and 2.8 per cent Muslims mentioned about these acts. Divorce is frequent among Muslims and they contact mullah directly who grants it. Here government laws are neither effective nor seem to be important. Christian have no provision for divorce and it is very rare among Hindus.

Generally, a widow or divorcee is married to a widower or divorcee. However, widower or divorced men marry unmarried women. If a divorced woman marries again, her children live with the new husband. If both have children from earlier marriage all live together. But if the woman has run away or has married someone else children live with the father. This is only when a widower is married to a divorced woman or widow.

Usual Form of Marriage: Monogamy

The usual form is monogamy, which is the norm even among the Muslims of high socio-economic standing. Muslims of lower class may have two wives. Though Islam permits four wives, but such cases are not seen.

Though among Hindus, single wife is considered ideal, yet for some reasons one may have more than one wife. It is found that usually those who have more than one wife, the wives live separately and marriage is solemnised with only one. The second one is just a keep belonging to a lower class family. Such cases are very few.

If a Hindu wife is sterile, sometimes she herself advises her husband to bring a second wife and such marriages have actually taken place. But at times, the situation compels the husband to go in for a second marriage as an exception. Here is an instance. Mr A was married to a local woman whose entire family had gone to mainland except her younger sister who fell in love with the brother-in-law (*jija*) and eventually had sexual relationship with him. One day, they were caught by family folks in a compromising position. In order to save family honour and the girl's life, they married her to him. Thus, he became husband of two sisters simultaneously.

It is noticeable that in comparison to Muslim and Christian, more changes have come into Hindu marriage customs. Among Hindus themselves marriages are performed in different ways. Hindu customs have influenced Muslims and Christians and to a great extent Hinduisation has taken place. A common belief regarding aims of marriage is continuation of the family line and a recognised system of sexual satisfaction. No Hindu was conscious of religious purpose of marriage.

Family

Basically, India has a joint family system which can be traced back to Mahabharat period in 1000 B.C.[47] Generally, joint family is a typical Hindu characteristic which is prevalent throughout India and which is found in many non-Hindu communities too.[48] Joint families have six characteristics: common house, common kitchen, common expenditure, common social function, common right and property.[49] Generally, blood relatives of two or more generations live together. New judicial system, educational system, economic system, industrial-urban life have greatly affected, along with other institutions, joint family systems, too. Panniker[50], Dube[51], Kapadia[52], Kaldate[53], Agrawal[54], Morrison[55], Kurian[56], Goode[57], Basu[58], Berreman[59], Gough[60], Cohen[61], Mayer[62], Bose and Saxena[63], Shahani[64], Driver[65], Dumont[66], Kolanda [67], Abbi[68], Sharma[69], Malhotra and Sen[70], Desai[71], Srivastava[72], D'Souza[73], Ghosh[74], Chakki[75], Conklin[76], Shah[77], Acharya[78], and Kumar[79], in their studies of family have said that several factors are causing change in joint family system. Ishwaran[80] says that increasing nuclear family cannot survive without active cooperation and relationship with joint families. Though joint families still retain their importance yet many attacks caused by economic forces have affected them and this attack is perceptible through change in their structure.[81] It is evident that the family structure was built in Andaman under very unique and unfavourable circumstances. Here we make an attempt to analyse the present family system of early emigrant society.

Family Size

Indian families are characterised by their large size. Because of members of many generations living together, a joint family

Table 5.9
Description of Family Members

Religion	Number of Families	Number of Adults		Number of Minors		Number of Aged		Total		Average in Per Family			
(1)	(2)	(3)	(4)	(5)	(6)	(7)	(8)	(9)	(10)	(11)	(12)	(13)	(14)
Hindu	96 (55.2)	147 (51.9)	136 (48.1)	139 (53.9)	119 (46.1)	42 (55.3)	34 (44.7)	328 (53.2)	289 (46.8)	6.4	2.9	2.7	0.8
Muslim	72 (41.4)	110 (50.9)	106 (49.1)	135 (48.6)	143 (51.4)	30 (60.0)	20 (40.0)	275 (50.6)	269 (49.4)	7.5	3.0	3.9	0.6
Christian	5 (2.8)	9 (56.3)	7 (43.7)	3 (32.9)	4 (57.1)	2 (50.0)	2 (50.0)	14 (51.9)	13 (48.1)	5.4	3.2	1.4	0.8
Sikh	1 (0.6)	1 (100.0)	–	–	–	–	–	1 (50.0)	1 (50.0)	2.0	1.0	0.0	1.0
Total	174	267	249	277	266	74	54	618	572	6.8	2.9	3.1	0.8

Note: Figures in parentheses indicate per cent.

may have more than 100 members. The early emigrant families living in villages here are comparatively large. For examples there is a family in Garacharawa village of South Andaman with more than 70 members. They live together and have joint property, whereas in Port Blair town, which is just a part of Andaman isles, the size of joint families does not exceed 20-25 members. In this context, it is proper to analyse number and size of the respondents' families (see Table 5.9).

The average family size of the sample, 174, households comes to 6.8 per unit with 3.3 females and 3.5 males. Religion-wise the Muslims have larger families, with average 7.5 members per family followed by Hindus (6.4 members), and Christians (5.4). But 'size' alone may be a misleading indicator unless we go into the family types.

Types of Family

In this regard, it is proper to define different classifications of family, like joint, husband-wife, intermediate, nuclear, etc., so that no confusions or vagueness arises.

Joint Family

This implies married couples of at least two or more than two generations living under the same roof, such as parents and married children living with wife, etc., or two or more than two married couples, or two brothers with their wives living together.

Nuclear Family

Husband and wife, and their unmarried children or any unmarried brothers and sisters or either husband or wife living with his/her children in the same house.

Intermediate family husband and wife and their unmarried children with either mother or father or unmarried brother or sister or sister-in-law (wife's sister) living together.

Husband-Wife

Husband and wife living together without any other member.

Single

All those who live alone in a room or house.

Unusual Family

Small families, which are not common, e.g., a man living with his wife's sister or with his unmarried lover, etc.

During data collection for the present study, we came across two Hindu families of unusual type: a widower living with his deceased wife's sister and a Telugu-speaking man living with his lover and her younger sister in their house.

According to type of family, the largest number is nuclear (47.1%), followed by 28.7 per cent joint, 18.4 per cent intermediate and remaining 5.8 per cent of other types. Similarly, religion-wise too the nuclear family type is more prevalent. Among Hindus, 50 per cent are nuclear, 22.9 per cent joint, 21.9 per cent intermediate and remaining 5.1 per cent families includes single, husband-wife, and unusual types. Among Muslims, 43.1 per cent are nuclear, 37.5 per cent joint, 13.9 per cent intermediate and remaining families are of other types. Among Christians, 40 per cent nuclear, and single intermediate and joint families are 20 per cent each.

Since there is greater resemblance between the 'joint' and 'intermediate' family types, it can be said that both the main types that is, nuclear and joint is prevalent in almost equal proportion. As in the 'size' dimension, Muslims have relatively larger proportion of joint families; also what is not found in the general pattern is that the Christians have the lowest proportion of 'nuclear' families among the three major communities.

Regarding joint family, it is necessary to mention that there are families with two or more generations living together but in some families some members have separate kitchen or some members own individual movable or immovable property in addition to joint property. On such individual property, they have a monopoly right. Similarly, despite having separate kitchen they participate equally in all family activities and other rites. Besides, the senior-most member, who is *Karta* (Head), does not have any feeling of discrimination towards those who have separate kitchens. Married or unmarried member dependent on the family is taken full care of by the family.

Similarly, though nuclear families live separately from root family, having their own kitchen and individual property, yet collectively familial relationship with root family is maintained. Generally, parents arrange accommodation for married children and give them some part of the property also. In this way 'separation' (nuclear family) is amicable and there are generally no disputes on this score (part of the larger joint family).

The age structure of the families generally conforms the family types. Among Hindus, the average number of active (working) age members of 20-54 years is 2.9 per family. Members of young age group (1-19 years) and the old (55 years and above), on the average account for 3.5 persons per family. Obviously, 'dependent' members are in large number hence families are under economic pressure. The average numbers of Muslim family members under these groups are: 20-54 years 3; immature and old 4.5 per family. Sikh and Christian families have lesser number of dependants. In Christian families, the average number of members of 20-54 years is 3.2 and of children and old members 2.2.

On the whole, the distribution pattern works out as: 20-54 years 2.9; children 3.1 and old members 0.8 on the average per family.

Living together does have some benefits. An important question is what one thinks about joint family, because modern conditions seem to be against it. To find out respondents' view they were asked, "Would you like to live in a joint family?" A majority (53.4%) replied in negative and 46.6 per cent replied in affirmative. The response pattern more or less conforms to the prevalence of family types. The proportion of respondents actually living in joint families is 47.1 per cent and respondents favouring it are 46.6 per cent. Only 0.5 per cent living in such family disfavoured it. This may mean that they are actually tuned to the system, and perceived it as beneficial.

Sex Ratio

Historically and for obvious reasons, Andaman had a very adverse sex ratio, that is, there were far too less females as compared to males. Though, the ratio gradually increased over the years, it still continues to be the most adverse among all states of India. The 1971 census reported a sex ratio of 1000:644. But the aggregate figure could be highly misleading in relation to the early emigrant society, particularly. Evidently, the aggregate reflects the presence of a very large number of later day 'migrants' who have come here in search of employment or on transfer posting and live without their spouses/families.

Interestingly, our study shows that the sex ratio of 1000:926 among the 'early emigrants' is more favourable than those many states/regions in the mainland. Religion-wise, the ratio worked out are: Hindus 1000:8[81], Muslims 1000:978, Christian 1000:929, Sikhs 1000:1000. Certainly, it is more balanced among the Muslims and Christians. But on the whole the early emigrant society can be said to have overcome the distortions historically imposed. Age-wise sex ratio is as follows: 20-54 years 1000:933, 1-19 years 1000:960, 50 and above 1000:770. Thus, the age structure-wise sex ratios also indicate that the trend towards the narrowing of the differential.

Benefits of Joint Family

On a multiple response (rating) question most of the respondents (95.1%) perceived 'cooperation' as the main benefit of the joint family system. 83.9 per cent indicated 'saving' as a positive benefit, since men live in a group, the per head expenditure incurred in living separately is saved; 12.3 per cent felt that because of the presence of senior experienced members, children are brought up and socialised properly.

Regarding economy to be effected in the joint family, they feel that the income of the earning members of the family can be pooled that will give rise to more savings and investments, and also economic security.

It is important to point out here that *Karta* of joint family does not keep the family income. Every earning member gives a part of his income to *Karta* and rest remains as his individual income, which he may spend as he wishes.

Factors of Disintegration of Joint Family

Of course, there are numerous factors working against the joint family system here also. In early emigrant society of Andaman, family disintegration usually begins after marriage. Establishing a separate household after marriage is a strong tendency. It is heard and observed that after marriage the sons are more inclined toward the wife and her parental family.

All the respondents were of the view that family disputes are the main cause of the disintegration of the joint family. It is generally said that the dispute starts amongst female members. As usual, the conflict between the daughter-in-law and the mother-in-law is common and it becomes serious when the former is employed in a school or office. Such conflicts break the family in no time. Here is an example. Mr. A had love marriage with a Mopala Muslim who teaches in a school. Conflict cropped up between daughter-in-law and mother-in-law because the daughter-in-law could not coordinate between family chores, schoolwork and care of children. One day the conflict became serious. The mother-in-law rebuked the daughter-in-law who also retorted, accusing her father-in-law of drinking, which infuriated the mother-in-law and she slapped her. The earning daughter-in-law could not bear it and she too slapped her. When Mr. A came to know of it he beat his wife badly. Later, A thought it is better to live separately rather than having such unpleasant things every day and he moved elsewhere with his family.

Another cause of break-up of joint families is inter-religious or inter-group marriages, especially if the girl is considered to be of low status and the son marries her against the parents' wishes. In most such cases, he may have to leave the parental home. And such marriages are not very uncommon.

When both husband and wife earn, they are often not able to harmonise with the joint family. And if it is love marriage it is all the more difficult because they want to have a free private life. Elders of family do not like that daughter-in-law should go frequently out of the house, to cinema, hotels and enjoy life with her husband. Then on excuse of some petty difference or conflict the couple leaves the house. There are some men who want to live separately with their wives but do not have the courage to express it. So they get themselves transferred to some other island. If the wife is not working then there is no problem.

There are also instances when parents themselves divide the property after their sons' marriage and allow them to live separately. This saves family bickering and since division is not caused by any quarrel, goodwill prevails among brothers.

Head of Family

Generally, the father is the *karta* of the family and all members are responsible to him. When the old man becomes incapable to work, family authority passes on to the eldest son. The father commands full respect in the family and even when he becomes old, he is consulted in all family affairs. Mother is also paid special regard. Children are more attached to mother. After husband's death, if wife is capable, she actually wields family authority. In Mopala families' men have greater rights, whereas in other communities senior-most woman is given much importance in family matters.

In joint families too, male member is *karta* but in his absence, if there is an old woman in the family, she too may be *karta*. In this matter gender is not so important as age. Whosoever is senior and capable of bearing family authority does so.

Ghar Jawai (Son-in-Law Living with in-laws)

After marriage he who lives in his wife's place is called *ghar jawai*. Generally, such cases are seen where there is no male issue in the wife's family. In new emigrant society generally, he who has no relative in Andaman would live as a *ghar jawai*. For instance, Mr. A of Meerut works as assistant librarian and has timber business, is married to a local Hindu girl in whose family there is no male member except old parents. So, after marriage, he came to live in his wife's house.

Sometimes, when a boy wants to marry a girl without his parents' consent, but the girl's parents are willing, then the boy, after marriage, becomes *ghar jawai* and is taken as a family member. Mr. B, a Christian is a worker in the forest department. He fell in love with a Muslim girl. His family was not willing for the marriage but the girl's family was. So he left his house, married the girl, and came to her house to live.

There are some who became *ghar jawai* for financial gain or property. There are some exceptions where the girl's desire not to leave her parent's house is a cause. Though in early emigrant society, no one bothered if one is a *ghar jawai*, yet generally it is not considered good.

Parental Property

After father's death, movable and immovable properties are divided equally among sons. If mother is alive she becomes the owner. If property has not been divided before father's death, and mother is alive she is the owner and she divides it among her sons. Daughter's share depends on parents' wish. But generally, unmarried daughter is given a share. If the property is large and divisible, married daughter too is given a share.

Widow, *ghar jawai* and adopted son also get share in property. Not much conflict is seen over property. This depends on parents as to whom they give and how much they give. Property may also be given to maternal and paternal grand children, besides sons and daughters.

Fertility

High birth rate greatly affects society. Employment opportunities are shrinking because of increasing population, but for women employment too has much effect on fertility. According to a study, when a woman goes to work her fertility declines because of conflict between the roles of mother and worker which is resolved by women by reducing her fertility.[82] Studies made in developed countries show that only certain specific works done by women reduces fertility because in some profession work and childcare can be done simultaneously.[83]

Age at the time of marriage also affects fertility. Marriage at young age increases fertility.[84] Present study also attests it. Looking at the family size, data can be summarised that the fertility rate in the 'early emigrant society' is relatively high, the reason for this could be complex. We have tried to go into this aspect. In our study, we have analysed fertility rate of only women above 40 years from the 174 families. Excluding the women below forty was on the assumption that their fertility had not ended and those above forty or forty were included because their fertility had almost ended. Limiting the age status, we studied the cases of 62 Hindu, 49 Muslim, 4 Christian women and one Sikh woman which show that on an average a Hindu woman bears 5.9, Muslim 6.2, Christian 4.7 and Sikh 6.0 children. The average surviving rate is of 5.4 among Hindu, 5.6 in Muslim, 4.5 in Christian, and 5.0 in Sikh. This implies that the child mortality rate (per thousand) among Hindus is 91.9, among Muslims 108.7, among Christians 52.6, and among Sikhs 200.0 (see Table 5.10).

Table 5.10
Birth and Death Rates

Religion	*Total Birth*	*Average Birth per Woman*	*Total Alive*	*Average Alive*	*Death Rate per thousand*
Hindu	370	5.9	336	5.4	91.9
Muslim	306	6.2	276	5.6	108.7
Christian	19	4.7	18	4.5	52.6
Sikh	06	6.0	5	5.0	200.0*
Total	701	6.0	635	5.4	94.2

* There was only one Sikh women in the sample, therefore, it may create confusion.

An infant mortality rate (IMR) of mere 94.2 per thousand in early emigrant society may be regarded as appreciably lower in comparison with the entire country, the possible reason being adequate medical facility. The study area is located in south Andaman, which has five hospitals, twenty-one dispensaries, and one primary health centre. Being the only town on the islands, it also has the biggest hospital. Most deliveries take place in the hospital under the care of skilled doctors and nurses.

Generally speaking, the higher work participation by women and their larger representation in formal employment in government or private sector would have resulted in lower fertility rates. We have also noted that the marriage age for girls is also relatively higher; roughly similar to the urban middle class in mainland India, as compared to the rural communities.

Notes

1. Mathur, L.P., *History of Andaman and Nicobar Islands*, Ibid., p. 165.
2. N.A.I., Home Department, Judicial Branch, A Progs. No. 21, 15 January 1858.
3. Ibid., A Progs. No. 37, 7 May 1858.

4. Ibid., A Progs. No. 48, 19 May 1860.
5. Ibid., A Progs. No.48, 19 May 1860.
6. Mathur, L.P., Ibid., p. 166.
7. N.A.I., Home Department, Public Branch, A Progs. No. 89, December 1867.
8. Letter No. 1337, dated 31 October 1871 from Suptd. Port Blair to Govt. of India.
9. N.A.I., Home Department, Judicial Branch, A Progs. No. 76, April 1872.
10. Ibid., A Progs. No. 75, August 1874.
11. Ibid., A Progs. No. 80, August 1874.
12. Ibid., A Progs. No. 9, August 1881, quoted by Mathur, L.P., Ibid., pp. 167-168.
13. N.A.I., Home Department, Port Blair Branch, A Progs. No. 9, August 1881.
14. Ibid., A Progs. No. 74, June 1890.
15. Ibid., A Progs. No. 133, September 1891.
16. Administration Report, 1886-87, p. 48.
17. For details of Crime, see, Mathur, L.P., Ibid., pp. 169-170.
18. N.A.I., Home Department, Port Blair Branch, A. Progs. No. 28-40, July 1906, quoted by Mathur, L.P., Ibid., p. 170.
19. *The Andaman and Nicobar Manual*, Published by Authority, Calcutta, Suptd. of Govt. Printing, India, 1908, p. 178, Part I, Chapter XX.
20. Ibid.
21. Ibid., p. 179.
22. Ibid., p. 180.
23. *Gazetteer of India, 1908*, p. 204.
24. Ibid., p. 204.
25. Ibid., p. 205.
26. Serial No. 21A, S.S.O. No.1, dated 30.1.1909; Serial No.185 of Amendment slip to the *Andaman and Nicobar Manual*, No. 8 of 1916-17, 30 January 1917.
27. *Gazetteer of India*, p. 181, Part I. Chapter XX, Birth, Deaths and Marriage, *The Andaman and Nicobar Islands*, 1908.
28. Kapadia, K.M., *Marriage and Family in India*, (Hindi edition by K.K. Rawat) Motilal Banarasidas, Delhi, 1977, p. 173.

29. Ibid., p. 202.
30. Polly, W.H., *Encyclopaedia of Religion and Ethics*, Vol. 7, p. 433.
31. Merehant, K.T. *Changing Views on Marriages and the Family*, Madras, B.G. Paul and Co., 1935.
32. Desai, G.B., "Women in Modern Gujarati Life", unpublished thesis, University of Bombay, 1945.
33. Ghurye, G.S., *Caste and Class in India*, Bombay, Popular Book Depot, 1950; *Family and Kin*, Bombay, Popular Book Depot, 1955.
34. Kapadia, K.M., "Views and Attitudes of University Graduates in the Hindu Community, on Marriage and Family Relationships, in *Sociological Bulletin*, Vol. 3, No. 1, March 1954; "Changing Patterns of Hindu Marriage" in *Sociological Bulletin*, Vol. 3, No. 2, September 1954; "Changing Patterns of Hindu Marriage and Family'", in *Sociological Bulletin*, Vol. 4, No.2, September 1955; *Marriage and Family in India*, Bombay, Oxford University Press, 1958; "The Family in Transition", in *Sociological Bulletin*, Vol. 8, No. 2, September 1959.
35. Shah, B.V., "Gujarat College Students and Selection of Bride", in *Sociological Bulletin*, Vol. XI, 1962.
36. Mathew, A., "Expectation of College Students Regarding Their Marriage", in *Journal of Family Welfare*, Vol. 12, No. 3, March 1966.
37. Cormack, M.L., *The Hindu Women*, Bombay, Asia Publishing House, Indian Edition, 1961.
38. Ross, A.D., *The Hindu Family in Its Urban Setting*, Canada, University of Toronto Press, 1961.
39. Sharayu Bal and Varnarase, S.J., "Attitude of College Girls Towards Marriage", in *Journal of the S.N.D.T. Women's University*, Bombay, Vol. 3, 1966.
40. Kanan, C.T., *Inter-caste and Inter-community Marriage in India'* Bombay: Allied Publishers Pvt. Ltd., 1963.
41. Mahajan, A., "A Study of Attitudes of Women Students Towards Mate Selection", in *Journal of Family Welfare*, Vol. XII, No. 1, September 1965.
42. Fonseca, M., *Counselling for Marital Happiness*, Bombay, Manaktalas, 1966.
43. Hate, C.A., *Changing Status of Women in Post-Independence India*, Bombay, Allied Publishers Pvt. Ltd. 1969.
44. Kapoor, P., *Marriage and the Working Women in India*, Delhi, Vikas Publications, 1970.

45. Mehta, Rama, *The Western Educated Hindu Women*, Bombay, Asia Publishing House, 1970.
46. Das, Man Singh, "A Cross-Cultural Study of Intercaste Marriage in India and the United States", in *International Journal of Sociology of the Family: A Special Issue of Intermarriage in a Comparative Perspective*, Vol. 1, May 1971.
47. Karve, I., *Kinship Organization in India*, Deccan College Research Institute, Poona, Asia Publishing House, Bombay, 1953, p. 10.
48. Kapadia, Ibid., p. 243.
49. Karve, I., Ibid., p. 10.
50. Pannikar, K.M., *Hindu Society at Cross Road*, Bombay, Asia Publishing House, 1955.
51. Dube, S.C., *Indian Village*, London: Routledge and Kegan Paul Ltd., 1955.
52. Kapadia, Ibid., 1966.
53. Kaldate, Sudha, "Urbanisation and Disintegration of Rural Joint Family", *Sociological Bulletin*, 1961, 11 (1&2).
54. Agrawal, B.R., "Caste and Joint Family in a Mobile Commercial Community", *Sociological Bulletin*, 1955, 4(2); "Nature and Extent of Social Change in Mobile Commercial Community (Study of Change in Family and Marriage Patterns)", *Sociological Bulletin*, 1961, 11(1-2).
55. Morrison, W.A., "Family Types in Badlapur: An Analysis of a Changing Institution in Maharastrian Village", *Sociological Bulletin*, 8 (1959).
56. Kurian, George, *The Indian Family in Transition: A Case Study of Kerla Syrian Christians*, Hague: Mouton, 1961.
57. Goode, W.J., *World Revolution and Family Patterns*, Glencoe, Free Press, 1963.
58. Basu, T.R., *The Bengal Peasant from Time to Time*, New York, Asia Publishing House, 1962.
59. Berreman, G.D., *Hindus of the Himalayas*, Berkeley and Los Angeles, University of California Press, 1963.
60. Gough, K.B., "Caste in Tanjore Village", (ed.) Beach, *'Aspects of Caste in South India, Ceylon and N.W. Pakistan'*, Cambridge, 1960.
61. Cohen, B.S., "Chamar Family in a North Indian Village: A Structural Contingent", *Economic Weekly*, 13, 1961.
62. Mayer, A.C., *Caste and Kinship in Central India*. Berkeley and Los Angeles, University of California Press, 1960.

63. Bose, A.B. and Saxena, P.C., "Composition and Size of Rural Joint Household", *Indian Journal of Social Research*, 1965.
64. Shahani, S., "The Joint Family: A Case Study", *The Economic Weekly*, 1961.
65. Driver, B.D., "Family Structure and Socio-Economic Status in Central India", *Sociological Bulletin*, Vol. II, 1962.
66. Dumont, Louis, "Caste, Racism and Stratification: Reflections of a Social Anthropologist", *Contributions to Indian Sociology*, No. V, Oct. 1961.
67. Kolanda, P.M., "Region, Caste and Family Structure: A Comparative Study of the Indian Society", in Milton Singer and Bernard S. Cohen (eds.), *Structure and Changes in Indian Society*, Chicago: Aldine Publishing Co., 1968; R.I. Crane (ed.) *Regional Differences in India Family Structure,* "Regions and Regionalism in South Asians Studies: An Exploratory Study, Duke University Programme in Comparative Study in Southern Asia", Symposium Papers, 1967.
68. Abbi, B.L., "Urban Family in India", *Contribution to India Sociology*, New Series, 1969, No. 3.
69. Sharma, J., "The Nuclearization of Joint Family Households in West Bengal", *Man in India*, 1964.
70. Malhotra and Sen, "A Comparative Study of the Socio-Economic Characteristics of Nuclear and Joint Household", *Journal of Family Welfare*, Vol. II, No. 2, 1964.
71. Desai, I.P., *Some Aspects of Family in Mahuva*, Bombay, Asia Publishing House, 1964.
72. Srivastava, Ram P., "Family Structure and Change Among the Overseas Indians with Special Reference to Indian Immigrant Families in British Columbia", in George Kurion (ed.) *Family in India: A Regional View*, The Hague Mouton, 1974.
73. D'Souza, Victor, "Family Types and Industrialization in India", in George Kurian (ed.) op. cit.
74. Ghosh, B.R., "Changes in the Size and Composition of the Household Brought About by Urbanization", in George Kurian (ed.) op. cit.
75. Chekki, D.A., "Modernization and Social Change: The Family and Kin Network in Urban India", in G. Kurian (ed.) op. cit.
76. Conklin, George, H., "Emerging Conjugal Role Patterns in a Joint Family System: Correlates of Social Change in Dharwar, India", *Journal of Marriage and Family*, 35 (November 1974).

77. Shah, A.M., *The Household Dimension of the Family in India: A Field Study of Gujarat Village and a Review of Other Studies*, Berkeley: University of California Press, 1974.
78. Acharya, H., "Some Possible Variation in Family Types in Gujarat", in George Kurian (ed.) op. cit.
79. Kumar, Joginder, "Family Structure in Hindu Society", in George Kurian (ed.) op. cit., 1974.
80. Ishwaran, K., "The Interdependence of Elementary and Extended Family", in George Kurian (ed.) op. cit.
81. Kapadia, Ibid., p. 275.
82. "Women: Mother or Worker?" (A Study under I.L.O. World Employment Programme), *People*, Vol. 6, No. 3, 1979, p. 10.
83. Ibid., p. 10.
84. "Survey Shows Fertility Decline", *People*, Vol. 6, No. 3, 1979.

6 Economic and Occupational Life

In this chapter, an attempt has been made to describe economic and occupational life of the early emigrants, together with a brief historical background of the early period of penal settlement establishment. It describes the present sources of livelihood of early emigrants, the family as the economic unit, the working population, their occupational status and mobility, economic hierarchy, family income-expenditure, material standard of life, housing and living conditions and other relevant features.

During the early period of colonisation, prisoners were generally put to clear forest and raise buildings for the colony.[1] Gradually, all those capable of any profitable occupation were granted permission to do so.[2] For proper administration of the penal settlement, the prisoners were put in different categories. Initially, most would be put under class III.[3] Later, on the basis of record of conduct during prison sentence they were promoted to class II and appointed as *tindal* (warder) to keep an eye on class III prisoners. On satisfactory performance in the role, after a specific period they were promoted to class I category and declared 'self-supporters'. Such persons were given financial assistance by the government for six-months to enable them to attain this status. They were given agricultural land and assistance for raising cattle and poultry. A self-supporter prisoner could do any of the following: catching fish, farming, selling milk and butter, making sweets, work as cobbler, clerk, orderly, boat-rowing, compounder, etc. There was administrative restriction on occupational choice and this was dictated by the labour/manpower needs of the penal settlement. Facts suggest that in the beginning permission and opportunity was given to prisoners to take up only low class occupations. They were also compelled to take up professions contrary to their hereditary occupation. Looking at 1864 data, we find that according to Napier's estimate out of total 3,382 prisoners, 2,020 (59.7%) were employed in clearing the forest.[4] Gradually the colony's requirements increased and around 1890 a significant number of prisoners were employed as industrial labourers, forest felling, logging and export of timber/fuel, rope making – mostly forest-based activities. In the beginning, besides agriculture and unskilled labour there was no opportunity for choosing any other occupation. As the number of prisoners and free population increased in the settlement, its requirements also increased. It was also decided that the colony should become self-reliant. This naturally increased opportunities for work and employment.

Table 6.1 gives the work allotment pattern in the early phase of the colony (1881-1901).[5]

The figures show that most prisoners were used as coolie or domestic hand. British officers were charged with the responsibility to cut down the expenditure on the maintenance of the prison establishment. That is why, they were put to such works that would develop as resources of the island.

The self-supporters contributed significantly to the development of the colony by reclamation of forestland for agriculture. In 1881, the cleared land was 10,421 acres, which in 1905 increased 25,189 acres. Similarly, the cultivated area of 6,775 acres in 1881 increased to 10,364 acres by 1905.[6] As prisoner population increased so also the demand for food grains. Remarkable development of agriculture was achieved in southern parts of Port Blair and thousands of prisoners were placed in new villages/settlements. The *Choudharis* and *Chowkidars* in these villages were paid a fixed salary. A considerable part of arable land was allocated for vegetable cultivation, and tea, coffee, cocoa and coconut plantations, besides rice and other cereals.

Table 6.1
Nature of Employment

Nature of Employment	*Years*		
	1881	*1891*	*1901*
Supervising	701	688	1,118
Commissariat	207	186	162
Medical	124	203	125
Marine	562	744	290
Forest	56	438	706
Cultivation	144	562	616
Manufacturing	797	941	1,098
Cloth	631	242	252
Coolies and domestic servants	3,954	4,083	3,642

Although government encouraged spread of agriculture, yet growth remained comparatively slow for which Sen[7] has given three seemingly correct causes: the prisoner was not the land owner; government made little effort to create market for surplus production; and many prisoners did not know farming. Certainly, under such circumstances, the desired development of agriculture was not possible.

Unsatisfactory pace of agricultural development led to fundamental changes in government policy in the second decade of the twentieth century. The 1921 declaration to change the penal settlement into a free residential settlement gave a boost to agricultural development. Persons fulfilling certain conditions were conferred land ownership right.

In the following years, the economy of the penal settlement underwent drastic change, especially during Colonel Ferrar's tenure (1923-31) with the change in the administrative character of the colony, government service emerged as an important occupational category. In the 1931 census report 625 persons of local born community (early emigrants) were classified as earning members out of them 53.8 per cent were government employees in different capacities, 40 per cent were earning their livelihood from agriculture and the rest were engaged in other activities (e.g., fisheries, trade, rural handicraft, etc).[8] Moreover, it may not be improper to say that the 'locals' were mostly employed in lower cadre posts.

During Japanese occupation (1942-45), these islands were totally cut off from the rest of India. There was acute scarcity of food due to wartime dislocations. The prisoners were put to agricultural work day and night. The Japanese utilised entire arable land of south Andaman, both plain and hilly, for potato and tapis (generally known as Malayali potato) farming. Local people were terrorised into work and those who disobeyed were killed. Self-sufficiency did come but at pain of coercion unleased by the Japanese army, so that people wanted to forget the agricultural lesson taught by the Japanese, as soon as their occupation ended. They abandoned agriculture except few. Even today, abandoned fields can be seen at different places.

We find very little agricultural reform until independence. Because of opening of forest and other governments departments, early emigrants abandoned agriculture. The 40 per cent farmers' population in 1931, declined to mere 29 per cent. Early emigrants sold their agricultural land to new emigrants and purchased property in Port Blair. Further, decline of agriculture would have been there but for the arrival of new emigrants and formation of new agricultural settlements. Agricultural development picked up once again. For most of new emigrants, displaced persons from Pakistan, Bangladesh, Sri Lanka and Burma agriculture became main occupation.

Occupational structure data of the 1951 census report again indicated decline in agricultural employment with only 29 per cent employed in agriculture and plantation. This includes not just early emigrants but also new emigrants and refugees from Burma and other places. It is indicated that early emigrants in a good number took new occupations abandoning agriculture. Those employed in agriculture took to cash cropping like coconut and arcenut. With the opening of educational institutions locally and facility of education on the mainland, many became qualified and secured employment in different government departments, and other establishments.

If we look at the occupational bases of working population after 1951, we find that the number of people working in agriculture sector declined rapidly up to 1971.

For occupational analysis of population, it is pertinent to understand chief sources of livelihood in the islands. More than 90 per cent[9] land of this Union Territory is covered with forests*. Surrounded by sea on all sides the isles are full of marine wealth. Different kinds of fish, crocodile, shark, tortoise, shellfish and rock wealth are available in abundance. Sweet water fish are almost negligible. Fish from sea and river streams is the staple diet of the people. Fishing has great potentiality here. Absence of traditional fishermen on the islands is one of the constraints in exploration of fishing resource.

Only fishery and forestry and industries based on them cannot be the basis of a self-reliant economic system. On account of transportation costs, local timber cannot compete in Mumbai and Chennai markets. Regarding mineral wealth N.V. Portman in his geological survey had collected specimens of iron, copper, sulphur and chromium. Later Mallet[10] came here to further this work but could not find any significant concentration of minerals. It is believed that the Japanese during their occupation made extensive survey of minerals, and discovered

---

* According to National Council of Applied Economic Research study 'Techo-economic Survey of Andaman and Nicobar Islands' (New Delhi, 1972) this figure is only 78 per cent.

deposits of coal, iron, and precious stones.[11] As yet no exploitation of minerals has taken place; either attempts are incomplete or minerals just do not exist. Although in recent years, Oil and Natural Gas Commission has discovered oil and gas deposit in the sea, 19 kms away from Port Blair, yet production is yet to begin.

Although population density is low (in 1981, 23 per square kilometre) yet pressure on agricultural land is very high. Want of irrigation facilities has widespread adverse effect on crops. Climatic conditions encourage crop diseases, pests and insects. Scarcity of arable land is apparent and food production is insufficient for the local population.[12]

It is but proper to discuss here local industries and their potentialities. Raw material, electric supply, minerals and wide market for produced goods are four primary factors for industrial prosperity of any place and all of them are lacking in Andaman, whose major raw materials are forest timber, coconut, arcenut, sea shells, mother of pearl, etc. Non-availability of raw material for heavy industries foreclose such development. Since there is no correlation between agrarian economic system and cottage industries Port Blair's population, especially the early settlers swarm over service employment avenues. Most of such employment is in government sector. Many early emigrants and others indulge in illegal supplying of Amber and Havabil.[13] At present, employment opportunities both in government and non-government sectors are severely limited, causing tension between early and new emigrants and other sections of population who are organised as interest groups on this issue. Highest government post is held by the officer sent from the mainland who qualifies the all India competitive examinations. On middle positions too, officials are sent from mainland. Members of 'early emigrant' segment are given preference in appointment to class III and IV posts, or rather these posts are reserved for them. Government jobs, however, are main attraction for majority of the people.

There is a rising demand that 'locals' should be appointed in class I and class II posts or other service positions but the government has its own reasons such as[14]:

(1) lack of sufficient trained personnel in the islands themselves, and
(2) an unstated government policy decreeing the wisdom of putting an outsider incharge of local affairs (the Home Ministry's reported fear, apparently, is that the locals may not be sufficiently objective and ruthless in matters of decision affecting local administration).

Early emigrants argue that only their people should be appointed on high posts as they understand local problems and would find quick and proper solution. They also argue that there is no lack of educated and capable people among them.

To verify the arguments of local people, we can put here the educational qualifications of the respondents and their family members (see Table 6.2).

Table 6.2

Distribution of the Respondents and their Family Members According to their Educational Qualifications

Educational Level	*Female*	*Male*	*Total*
Less than High School	225(64.8)	228(74.8)	453(69.5)
High School and Intermediate	92(27.4)	61(20.0)	156(23.9)
Graduate	25(7.2)	15(4.9)	40(6.1)
Post-graduate	2(0.6)	-	2(0.3)
Ph.D.	-	1(0.3)	1(0.2)
Total	347(53.2)	305(46.8)	652(100.0)

Note: Figures in parentheses are percentages.

It is clear from the table above that the educational level of the majority (69.5%) of the members is low, that is, below the level of high school or equivalent. Only 23.9 per cent of that are educated up to high school or intermediate level. About 60 per cent are graduates and only 0.3 per cent have post-graduate qualification. Only one male person has received Ph.D. degree. On the whole, we may conclude that the respondents do not have the educational qualifications for the higher posts.

Occupational Pattern of Early Emigrants

As described earlier, agriculture was the main occupation of most of the early emigrant to begin with, but in due course of time it changed to service and at present their descendants in Port Blair town are employed in service sector. This is also corroborated by the data gathered from the sample households about the occupational shift (inter-generational occupational mobility) from their father and grandfather.

When the respondents were enquired about the occupations of their grand parents, they acknowledge that 33.4 per cent of them do not know about their grandfather's occupation but all of them guess that they would have been involved in agriculture. Most of the remaining said it was agriculture (63.8%), followed by trade (15.5%), government service (13.8%) and other occupations like butcher, washerman, weaver, blacksmith, tailor, and earthen-pot maker (6.9%).

It is an interesting fact that whereas 63.8 per cent of respondents' grandfather's occupation was agriculture, in their father's case, it declined to mere 27.2 per cent, and the proportion of those in service rose to 54.4 per cent and of those in trade to 11.8 per cent. The remaining 6.6 per cent were in other occupations like washer-man, blacksmith, labour, and tailoring, etc. (see Table 6.3).

This trend in inter-generation occupational mobility was further strengthened and in respondents' own generation (N=161) representation in agricultural occupation has been reduced to 0.6 per cent only. We have already said that early emigrants are heavily inclined toward service. It may be observed that, because of low educational standard, most of early emigrants are employed on class III and IV posts. Our data indicate, that most people, even at present are working as clerks

(26.7%), or technician (24.4%) or in various class IV posts (10.6%). In the teaching profession (9.3%), most respondents are in intermediate section or below. Of course, we have to keep in mind that the respondents are mainly town dwellers of Port Blair, where most of the early emigrants have concentrated, and their service orientation has been a powerful factor in this regard.

Table 6.3

Distribution of the Respondents According to their Fathers' and Grandfathers' Occupation

Occupation	*Grandfather*	*Father*
Business	18(15.5)	20(11.7)
Agriculture	74(63.8)	46(27.2)
Service	16(13.8)	92(54.4)
Other Occupations (butcher, washerman, weaver, blacksmith, labourer, painter, etc.)	8(6.9)	11(6.6)
Total	116(66.6)	169(97.1)
Do not know	58(33.4)	5(2.9)
Grand Total	174(100.0)	174(100.0)

Note: Figures in parentheses are percentages.

An important fact in context of occupational analysis is that no one from early emigrant society in Port Blair works as a sweeper. All sweepers employed in Port Blair municipal board came from new emigrant society. It has already been pointed out that originally a significant number of early emigrants belonged to depressed castes. During penal settlement period, some convicts were forced to work against their caste status. Yet at present no one wants to go for such occupations. Apparently, the whole context and course of development of this former penal settlement offered many opportunities to the early emigrants' descendants to run away from the 'unclean' occupations, and change their unclean caste identity.

Material Life-style

Residential Condition

Housing problem is not confined to India and her cities rather it is a global problem[15] and it is becoming graver with greater urbanisation. It would be appropriate to say that India's future is bleak because here the rate of population growth is much more than the housing construction rate.[16]

Although different classes of people live in Port Blair town, yet houses here are almost of the same type. Average standard of housing here is higher than that of Indian cities because of comparatively better economic condition of the people[17], and good quantity of locally available building material used for walls and roofing.[18] To the extent possible locally available materials are used in house building. In Andaman isles, in villages mostly grass, leaves, wood, bamboo and reeds are used for walls and roofing. In Port Blair town, wood is used for walls and corrugated tin sheets for roofing. Although corrugated iron sheets are not locally manufactured yet the government maintains the supply and these are much in use in Port Blair town and villages. Building timber used to be easily available and relatively cheap too.

Wall Materials

In this territory, as far as possible, the locally available materials have been found used for the construction of houses. Heavy rains, tropical sun and stormy weather have greatly influenced residential pattern of the islands. The structure and style of houses is environmentally appropriate. Plinth of the houses built on raised elevation keeps the interiors dry even in wet weather and free from snakes and other insects coming up abundantly during rains.

All houses built during the early period of penal settlement are on Burmese pattern. Roofs are sloping, and mostly made of tiles. Iron and cement sheets for roofing became popular later in Port Blair town, although these are not suitable for residential houses because tropical sun makes such houses uncomfortable. Actually the reason for popularity of corrugated tin sheet is its lasting quality and protection against heavy rain. Almost every house in Port Blair town has walls of building-timber. Brick walls are rarely seen. Use of cement and bricks is on the increase in government buildings and also in houses of some well-off people. Preference to bamboo and building timber houses is given to mud and brick houses because of earthquake proneness of the islands. Style of existing houses is similar to that of houses in hilly regions of mainland.

It will not be wrong to infer that almost all early emigrant own houses. In the sample, 85.6 per cent have their houses. Only those do not have own house who are either young and have separated or live away from their family.

Most houses have bedroom, kitchen, bathroom and lavatory. In the houses of upper class persons, one may find a guest room, dining room, dressing room, study room, *puja* room and store, etc. Community-wise housing status of the respondent is as follows:

Hindu houses have maximum number of bedrooms (average of 2.70 per family), followed by Muslim houses (2.69 per family), Christian (2.25), and Sikh (2.00). Though Christian houses have lesser bedrooms yet their average size is largest (262.22 square feet). From the point view of entirety, on average early emigrant utilise 2.68 rooms of their houses as bedroom whose average size is 154.54 square feet per room. Every Sikh house has one guest room of average size of 112 square feet. Similarly, every Christian house has dining room followed by 15.6 per cent Hindu houses. It is strange that none of the Muslim houses has a separate dining room possibly because of large families. Except Hindus, followers of all other religions on an average have one kitchen. Only 3.1 per cent Hindu and 1.4 per cent Muslim houses have no separate kitchen rooms. Use of rooms as store is very rare, possibly because in comparison to mainland there is little risk of theft here. Generally, houses have verandah and balcony, especially in double storey houses. As an exception some houses, mostly of Hindus, have study and dressing room also because economically they are better off in comparison to followers of other religions.

Nearly cent per cent houses have fixed bedrooms. Regarding guest and drawing room, it is significant that all Sikh houses have them, followed by 75 per cent Christian, 62.5 per cent Hindu, and 31.9 per cent Muslim houses. All Sikh and Christian houses have kitchen room.

The houses lack adequate sanitary latrine facility. Whatever there are, are of crude type. Actually, 6.9 per cent Muslim and 4.2 per cent Hindu houses have no lavatory facility. They go to seashore or to their own orchards for defecation. Generally, they are people with low economic status. Only 8 per cent houses have permanent arrangement of lavatory with flush system. Rest of lavatories are in a bad shape, though cleaned by municipal board sweeper on daily basis. Private sweepers are not available.

Similarly, 4.2 per cent of Muslim and 3.1 per cent of Hindu houses do not have bathrooms. Men usually bathe outside and women either in the kitchen corner or in lavatory itself. All Sikh houses have verandah or balcony, but among the other communities, 40.6 per cent Hindu, 25 per cent Christian, and 27.8 per cent Muslim houses have these features. Separate *puja* rooms are found in very few houses only. Usually in the bedroom itself, there are idols or pictures. Most of the Muslims perform *namaz* in the bedroom. Only 14.6 per cent Hindu and 4.2 per cent Muslim houses have such prayer rooms.

Nearly 11.6 per cent of respondents' houses have no private water connection. Only 15 per cent houses have wells and remaining use water supplied by municipal water tankers. A significant fact about housing conditions is that all those who own houses are content with the housing facility while 16.7 per cent living in rented houses are not.

Table 6.4

Per House Average Rooms and Space in Square Feet

	Hindu	*Muslim*	*Sikh*	*Christian*
Bed Room	2.70 (150.5)	2.69 (150.3)	2.00 (112.0)	2.25 (262.2)
Living Room	0.62 (190.7)	0.33 (154.3)	1.00 (112.0)	0.75 (204.3)
Dining Room	0.15 (148.8)	–	–	0.50 (102.5)
Kitchen	0.98 (136.3)	1.00 (108.2)	1.00 (70.0)	1.00 (54.4)
Terrace	0.51 (83.7)	0.37 (140.0)	–	2.25 (25.0)
Store	0.45 (99.9)	0.29 (57.2)	–	0.50 (44.5)
Bathroom	1.01 (29.3)	1.02 (23.7)	1.00 (16.0)	1.00 (18.8)
Lavatory	1.04 (16.7)	1.00 (17.8)	1.00 (16.0)	1.00 (19.8)
Dressing Room	0.02 (72.0)	–	–	–
Study Room	0.06 (120.2)	0.01 (100.0)	–	–
Prayer Room	0.14 (66.9)	0.04 (68.3)	–	–
Guest Room	–	0.01 (100.0	–	–

Note: Figures in parentheses denote square feet.

Table 6.5

Average Rooms and Average Size per Family

	Number	*Square Feet*
Bed Room	2.68	154.54
Living Room	0.50	180.32
Dining Room	0.10	140.94
Kitchen	0.99	122.29
Lavatory	1.02	17.21
Bathroom	1.01	26.63
Terrace	0.44	102.69
Store	0.38	84.86
Prayer Room	0.09	67.11
Study Room	0.04	117.28
Dressing Room	0.01	72.00

To conclude, comparatively speaking the housing conditions are better, yet this can definitely be said that, the house may be called sanctuary of family life and its conditions are fully related with family health.[19] Therefore, essential aim of a house is to provide comfort, health and entertainment that make home and where early form of society, family life develops.[20] From this point of view, it may be said that insufficient arrangement for lavatory and bath, haphazard interior setting of the houses create unhealthy conditions. Moreover, generally speaking, the houses are not well maintained and many of them are in a bad state.

Income*

Although from the standpoint of their position in the occupational hierarchy, most early emigrants' status is low, yet their economic condition is comparatively sound because of other sources of income like rents and agricultural income in addition to salary (see Table 6.6).

Table 6.6

Distribution of the Respondents According to Other Sources of Income

Sources	*Hindu (N=96)*	*Muslim (N=72)*	*Sikh (N=1)*	*Christian (N=4)*	*Others (N=3)*
House Rent	83 (86.4)	61 (84.7)	1 (100.0)	4 (100.0)	149 (86.1)
Residential Plot	37 (38.5)	26 (36.1)	1 (100.0)	1 (25.0)	65 (37.6)
Agricultural Land	25 (26.0)	8 (11.1)	- (25.0)	1 (25.0)	34 (19.6)
Plantation	23 (23.9)	12 (16.7)	1 (25.0)	1 (25.0)	36 (20.8)

Note: Figures in parentheses denote percentages.

Rent money is a significant part of family income since 86.1 per cent of respondents' own houses and 57.7 per cent have

* The data on income was collected some time in 1980s during first fieldwork.

rented rooms with and average additional monthly income of Rs 420.05. Among Christians, 25 per cent houses are rented out on an average monthly rent of Rs 300 each. Among Muslims 84.7 per cent have their own house and out of them 54.1 per cent have rented out accommodation and on the average receive monthly income of Rs 368.03 each. Among Hindus, 86.4 per cent own houses, out of them 61.4 per cent have rented income of Rs 438.82 each month. These figures show that income from rents has an important element in family income. Besides, produce from fields and orchards, like arcenut, coconut, banana and vegetables, etc., also add to family income. But, for non-availability of definite information, no clear idea can be given of the net addition to family income on this account.

The average monthly income of each family works out to Rs 1,433.38. Religion-wise, figure comes to Rs 1,784.5 for Christians, followed by Rs 1,588.89 for Hindus and Rs 1,220.88 for Muslims. Number of earning members in a family is also the highest among Christians (2.6%), followed by Hindus (2.23%) and Muslims (2.09%). On the whole sample population, the average number of working members in a family is 2.19 per cent.

Table 6.7

Economic Conditions

	Hindu	*Muslim*	*Sikh*	*Christian*	*All*
Per month average income (in Rs) (per family)	1,588.89	1,220.88	400.00	1,784.50	1,433.38
Average earner per family	2.23	2.09	1.0	2.6	2.19
Monthly per capita income (in Rs)	247.21	161.58	200.00	264.37	208.38
Monthly income of per earner (in Rs)	709.46	582.14	400.00	549.07	652.56
Average dependent member per earner	2.86	3.60	1.0	2.07	3.13

Per capita monthly income is highest among Christians (Rs 264.37) followed by Hindus (Rs 247.21), Sikhs* (Rs 200) and Muslims (Rs 161.58). On the whole, the per capita monthly income of members of early emigrant society is Rs 208.38.

On an average, monthly income per earning member is highest among the Hindus (Rs 709.46), followed by Muslims (Rs 582.14) and Christians (Rs 549.07).

The number of dependants per earning member is important since it provides a clearer picture of economic condition of the family. From this point of view, maximum number of dependants is among Muslims (3.60), followed by Hindus (2.86), and Christian (2.07). From the whole sample households, there are 3.13 dependants per earning member.

To conclude, Christians are better off than others, mainly because of more earners and lesser dependants. Conversely, the Muslims are economically the weakest among the three major communities, mainly because of a higher dependency ratio.

Income alone does not present the correct picture of economic condition of a people. Life-style and consumption patterns are also important in determining economic well-being of a society. Actual indicator of people's cultural attainment is their standard of living.[21] Here, we are mainly concerned with expenditure on satisfaction of the basic needs as also found in studies by Dandeker & Rath[22] and Wiebe[23], that it is a truism that the poorer the family the greater its expenditure on essentials like food and fuel, etc.

Looking at pattern of family expenditure, we find that a significant part is spent on basic necessities of life like food and vegetables and the minimum (0.7%) is spent on medicine and treatment. This does not mean that community health is very good but because medical treatment is free in the islands. Little is spent on housing because most people (86.1%) own houses. Religious ceremonies on rituals entail very little expenses

* There was only one Sikh household in the sample. Therefore, it cannot be regarded as representative of the community.

because such events are rarely held. Another significant item of expenditure is children's education on which on an average a family spends Rs 60.15 per month. The families pay attention to children's education, up to the intermediate level at least. However, very few go in for higher education.

Consumption of vegetables is rather small but it is substituted by fish, which is easily available. Due to scarcity of fresh milk, tinned milk is used. LPG cylinders are not available here[24] and wood is used for fuel.

People generally wear good clothes, especially when they go out. It was calculated that 6.9 per cent of total family expenditure is on clothes. The climate of the place however, does not require heavy and expensive clothing.

The majority of people eat betel leaves. Expenditure on alcohol is high. A high percentage of male population takes alcohol. The household expenditure pattern shows only 6.3 per cent on alcohol, betel and cigarettes. This appears to be underreported. We could see that almost all families consume alcohol. About 9.7 per cent of expenditure is on miscellaneous items, which includes marriage, social ceremonies, etc. Saving at 21.7 per cent of income indicates sound economic condition.

Sources of recreation, and entertainment are very few, and expenditure on it is 2.8 per cent, i.e., each family spends Rs 51.79 on it per month. The most important source of entertainment is cinema, which plays both positive and negative roles. It will not be wrong to quote here a local official of Anthropological Survey of India: "Adolescents here imagine mainland through films and imitate films in their manners and dress. It is only because of films that whether coming from high or low class, all young people fall in love pretty early." All families go to cinema for entertainment.

Radio too is an important and cheap source of entertainment. It broadcasts national, social, economic, educational and cultural activities along with song, music and sports items. A legacy of British Raj is that listening to BBC is popular among all age groups in most families. Port Blair station of All

India Radio broadcasts programmes in almost all important languages. From time to time sports competitions also provide entertainment, which is confined to men only.

A significant fact is that only 9.25 per cent respondents have taken life insurance policy. Actually, it has not been propagated and hence many are unaware of it.

Indebtedness

Despite apparently sound economic conditions, 17.3 per cent respondents have taken loans. With an average of Rs 11,776.67 per family, average debt on all indebted families comes to Rs 2,042.19. It is curious, that the same indebted households also save 21.7 per cent of total income. This implies that the borrowing may be mainly for 'investment'. An analysis of causes for debt shows that the majority of borrowers (56.7%) took loan for house building or repair and the average loan works out to Rs 10,288.23 per household. Though only 13.5 per cent respondent took loan for business, yet average debt is highest on this account (Rs 41,250). One such respondent borrowed Rs 80,000 for purchasing a truck, and 13.3 per cent have taken loan for purchasing two-wheelers for personal use with average debt of Rs 3,475 per household. One respondent has taken loan for agricultural development. Similarly, one has taken loan from cooperative society for purchasing a sewing machine. Only one person has taken loan of Rs 900 for marriage purpose from his General Provident Fund. Two other respondents are under debt for Rs 2,500 for personal expenses. Thus, on the whole, purely consumption loans are very few.

Sources of Loan

An important point is the source of borrowing or debt. Incurring debt from a moneylender or master/employer suggests exploitation. It is significant that none of the respondents has taken loan from such source. Loaning agencies are commercial banks (33.4%), cooperative bank (20%) and concerned departments.

Ownership of Material Goods

Ownership of material goods reflects life-style of the owner and also indicates the income level. In this connection, respondents were asked whether they owned car, scooter, radio, tape recorder, sofa, cycle, refrigerator, etc. The data available shows that most of families (84.5%) had radio or transistor, but only (22.4%) had a scooter or motorcycle. Though 17.8 per cent families had tape recorders (two-in-one) yet only 5.2 per cent had record player. Larger number of tape recorders may be attributed to the fact that local boys working in different ships, Indian and foreign, bring them home. Only 11.5 per cent families have cycles, because of hilly roads, cycle is not popular here. Only 3.4 per cent own cars, but only one family puts its car to personal use, and the remaining cars are being used as taxies. As far commercial vehicles, two families have a truck and jeep respectively. Though according to climatic conditions refrigerator is useful yet only two families have it.

On the whole, the picture of economic life in the 'early emigrant' community, as it emerges out of the figures on income and expenditure pattern (though 'dated' at this point of time, but relates to the actual reference period), shows that though the members may not be rolling in wealth, there is definitely no poverty or deprivation. It resembles a fairly good middle and lower middle class living. Whatever deprivations and tribulations their predecessors had undergone, the descendants of the 'early emigrants' have certainly gained from their better access to opportunities arising on these 'virgin' islands.

Notes

1. N.A.I., Home Department, Judicial Branch, A Progs. No. 21, 15 January 1858.
2. N.A.I., Home Department, Public Branch, A Progs. No. 4, 1 April 1864.

3. N.A.I., Home Department, Judicial Branch, A Progs., No. 21, 15 January 1958.
4. Mathur, L.P., Ibid., p.159.
5. Mathur, L.P., Ibid., p.160.
6. *The Imperial Gazetteer of India, 1901*, Ibid., p.207.
7. Sen, P.K., Ibid., pp.118-119.
8. *Census of India, 1931*, Ibid., p.30-31.
9. Andaman and Nicobar Islands Annual Report (1976-77).
10. Mallet, F.L., "On Some of the Mineral Resources of the Andaman Islands in the Neighbourhood of Port Blair", Res. G.S.I., Vol. XVII, 1884.
11. Sen, P.K., Ibid, p.46.
12. Report on World Agricultural Census 1970-71 in "A&N Islands Statistical Bureau (Agricultural Census Cell) A&N Administration", 1974, p.14.
13. For details about Hawabil and Amber, see *Yojana*, Vol. XX/13, 15 August 1976, Andaman and Nicobar, pp.50-51.
14. *Yojana*, Ibid., p.46.
15. Charles Abrams, "Man's Struggle for Shelter in an Urbanizing World: An Adaptation", *Current Thought Series*, No.2, Vakils, Feffer and Nimsons Pvt. Ltd., 1964, p.1.
16. *Indian News Magazine*, Vol. 14, No.5, September 12, 1971.
17. Sen, P.K., Ibid., p.147.
18. Mainly based on *Census Report of India, 1971*.
19. Mckintosh, J.N., *Housing and Family Life Preface*, London, 1952.
20. Mehta, A.B., *The Domestic Servant Class*, Popular Book Depot, Bombay, February 1960, p.115.
21. Joshi, Arvind Kumar, *The Clerks*, Vani Vihar, Varanasi, 1980, p.71.
22. Dandekar, V.M. and Rath, N., "Poverty in India", in *Economic and Political Weekly*, VI, January 2, 1971, pp.26-27.
23. Wiebe, Paul D., *Social Life in an Indian Slum*, Vikas Publishing House Pvt. Ltd., Delhi, 1975, p.95.
24. Note: LPG cylinders were not available at the time of fieldwork, that is, during 1980s. At present, the same is available for use.

7 Cultural Life

The cultural pattern of an 'artificial' or 'synthetic' society created in most unfavourable conditions out of men in exile almost exclusively was not likely to be a duplicate copy of that of the original society. Right at the beginning of the study, we have made the hypothesis that under such circumstances the society that forms in the long run is bound to lose some of its original features, even the essential ones, and undergo some sort of 'cultural genocide', or cultural impoverishment at least. On the other hand, the synthetic cultural pattern that evolves, after the tightly administered panel settlement changed its character, is bound to present interesting lessons in the process of development of a 'composite' culture.

Anthropological studies make *rites of passage* and 'social intensification' like pregnancy, birth, puberty, menopause, marriage, death, etc., as the basis to study the culture of a community. In any study of culture pattern of a community or society, customs, related to these events are important.[1] This chapter analyses cultural life and pattern of early emigrants, which not only confines to rites of passage but also includes various superstitions, religious beliefs and practice, magic totems, and so on. It may be noted that the basis for comparison is mainly the regional society from which the emigrants had come. And we proceed according to the life cycle. We understand that notion of impurity during menstruation are particularly strong in South India, when women are prohibited to enter kitchen to cook or fetch/touch drinking water and are generally confined to one room. This is not observed here, though there might be some exceptions. In fact, some members of this community exclaimed, how is it practicable? At the same time, it appears the coming of large number of new emigrants from the south and their cultural practices are affecting early emigrants of South Indian origin.

During pregnancy, women are generally well looked after. It is believed that happy and contented woman has a positive effect on baby. According to one's capacity, she is given nourishing food like milk and fruits, etc. She has to observe certain precautions during pregnancy like arduous work and lifting heavy objects. Generally, she continues domestic works until labour pain begins. From seventh month, she almost stops going out. During eclipse, she is asked to remain indoors. As in mainland India, it is believed that any exposure to eclipse has adverse effect on the foetus. There are no ritualistic prohibitions for husband to copulate with pregnant wife. Generally, a woman is taken for delivery to local government hospital. Although most deliveries in Port Blair town take place in hospitals, some deliveries, especially among Mopalas who consider home deliveries good, take place in home with the help of experienced old woman. But because of available medical facilities in government hospitals tendency of hospital delivery is increasing.

Normally, among Muslims, first childbirth takes place at the woman's parental house. Mopala Muslims celebrate first delivery. When the foetus is seven months old on fixed day seven or eight persons of girl's family go to the boys' place and have food. Then, the pregnant woman is taken to her parents' house by her in-laws. Among Hindus, she is sent to her parents if she desires or is called by them. Generally, parents take her to their house in the seventh month. Relatives bring *saree*, bangle, sweets, coconut and treating the pregnant *suhagin* (auspicious with living husband) fill her lap. The families in which she is not sent to her parents for delivery five or two *suhagin* woman (women with living husband) of the family perform this. South Indian Christians send her to her parents' house in the seventh month.

Here too, children are considered to be divine gifts and sons are preferred to daughters. The argument is that "son will continue family lineage, maintain parents, and would cremate them. Daughter belongs to someone else. She will go to her husband's place." Though sons are wished yet daughters are not despised. The Hindus consider first daughter as Lakshmi (goddess of wealth; auspicious) of the house.

If a child is not born after many years of marriage, the concerned people go for '*mannat*'. In South Point area of Port Blair town, there is a *mazar* (grave of a Muslim saint) which is famous for wish fulfilment and where people of all religions go. Preserving the ash of the grave is considered auspicious.

Generally, deliveries take place in hospitals which may be taken as indication of modernity, yet, in case of too much of labour pain or late delivery, diverse superstitious devices are also used for giving relief to the pregnant woman. In case of Hindus, they go to a Gurumurthi or Kamala Pandit who would give water or thread sanctified by some *mantra* for relief and quick delivery. The water is given to the pregnant woman to drink and the thread to wear. In case of Muslims, a Mulla's help is taken; he gives water, salt or two or three betel leaves treated with some esoteric formula or a talisman to be worn by her. Christians are given 'holy water' by priest to drink. Women of the family pray on prayer beads one of which is to be worn by the pregnant. Significantly, people of one religion may resort to 'superstition' solutions of other religions, like a Hindu going for 'holy water' or a talisman given by a mulla, or a Christian using devices of Hindus or Muslims.

At the time of delivery, the presence of close relations on the side of both spouses is considered good. Among the Hindu the baby's time of birth is given to Brahmin who casts horoscope; and without consulting him regarding planetary position the father would not look at the newborn. For example, a child born under *moola* planet is inauspicious whose malefic influence may kill one or both parents. Those believing in it, go in for *havan* and other rituals to nullify its malefic effects. For performing the rituals, the father brings earth and water from twenty-seven wells. Twenty-seven kinds of food grains and colours, etc., are used for the ritual. Parents are to stand outside the house in new clothes. A barber bathes them with water from a clay pot with twenty-seven holes in it. The new clothes worn by them are given to the barbar. Then the parents go in, clean themselves and wearing clean clothes sit for *havan* (fire sacrifice). A *thali* (plate) filled with mustard oil is placed before the parents. The baby's paternal aunt or maternal or paternal grandmother stands behind the parent with baby in her lap in such a manner that its reflection may be clearly visible in the oil. And this is how the father sees the baby for the first time. Then it is assumed that the malefic planet is pacified. Then friends and relatives are invited and treated with twenty-seven items of food. If the planetary 'anger' is very severe, even a cow may be gifted to the priest.

On the birth of a desired child people distribute sweets in rejoicing. As customary on mainland, people seeing the baby for first time give some gift in cash or kind, which, though not obligatory, is considered as good social behaviour.

There are divergent ways in which the cut piece of umbilical chord is disposed, specially, when the delivery takes place in the village home of the family. Such as Bhantus hang it in the house, and rural Christians bury it.

The newly born is suckled from the second day and if mother has no milk in her breasts the baby is given water with sugar. Baby is suckled so long it does not eat something. For want of fresh milk tinned milk is used.

Generally, the woman who has delivered does not go out for forty days, during which she is given different kinds of nutritious foods to regain health. She is given chicken soup for strength from the next day of delivery, which according to one's capacity is continued for 15 or 40 days. From the seventh day, a nourishing preparation (something like *achavani* in eastern UP) made of herbs, spices, dry fruits cooked in pure *ghee* is given to her. This mixture or spices is known as "spice of new mother" *(baccha wali aurat ka masala)* and is available in local market or from some family in the locality who process it. Mopalas call it 'legam'. This nourishing food is normally given daily for forty days. Other nourishing beverages and foods are also given for quick gain of energy and removal of body ache, etc. People of all religions usually consider such a woman unclean for forty days. During the period, she does not cook or do other work. Rather she does not do any thing. She lives separately confined to a room. Things are changing now because the working woman cannot observe these rules. Moreover, if the woman who has delivered is alone in the house she will naturally cook and do other chores.

Among Mopalas on the 40th day, a big feast is thrown called *'nalpad'* (meaning forty). People from both the spouses side are invited. Close relatives bring ornaments and gifts for the baby. It is the day of great rejoicing and feasting.

Christening

When a Mopala Muslim is born, honey is put in the mouth of the newly born. On birth of a child, a *namazi* (he who performs *namaz*) or mulla giving *azan* speaks 'Mohammed' in ear of male baby and 'Fatima' in case of female baby. Thus, it becomes their name and then on fortieth day *(nalpad)*, generally from father's side a name of his choice is given. Among other Muslims father's family folk give name of their choice and speak it in the baby's ear. In baby's christening the mother's family has no role.

Christians too give name to the newly born according to the choice of its father or his family. Then, the baby is taken to the church where the priest performs other rites. The same day some married couple is made the baby's godfather and godmother. The priest notes down the name of the baby and its parents in the church register. According to Christian custom at the age of five or six the child is baptised, when he is declared a full Christian and is taught religious norms. Certificate of membership of religion is also given which is produced as church membership at the time of marriage. Christian customs and traditions are controlled and regularised by priests and other ecclesiastical people according to rules of Christianity.

Among Hindus, at the time of birth, the astrologer, after making calculations, declares the zodiac number. Every zodiac number has certain letters and the parents give some name beginning with one of the letters of the zodiac number, though it is not strictly followed; the given name may begin with some other letter also. No date or time is astrologically fixed for naming ceremony, which can be done on any convenient day. Those who believe in it, may consult the priest. In this case, the day is fixed after one and a quarter month, or three months or five months. On the 21st day too, the baby may be put in the swing and mother may give a nickname.

Among Christians and Hindus on the day of naming, ceremonial feast is given to friends and relatives. May be that in the first child's case great celebrations are held and in the second child's case nothing is done because rules may be changed for convenience. Among Muslims, celebrations are held on the 40th day, which includes naming ceremony too. Though not obligatory, on this day Christians and Hindus may invite the priest and Muslims the mulla.

Tonsure Ceremony

As on mainland, here too custom of shaving birth hair of the child is prevalent. It is also observed among local Muslims. Generally among Hindus one and a quarter months, fifth, seventh, ninth or eleventh months after birth is considered auspicious for this or it is done after one, three, or five years. Months with even numbers like two, four, etc., are not considered auspicious; they are called pair months by early emigrants.

Among Hindus, we also see *chhathi mundan* (sixth day tonsure) as symbolic of pre-tonsure. On the sixth day after birth the barber touches the baby's nails and hair with razor and close family relatives are invited. On this auspicious day, the boy's paternal aunt's presence is considered necessary. After this, when the baby grows its nails are cut by family folks. On the sixth day, a white piece of paper and pen is put beneath the baby's pillow in the belief that the Almighty would write the baby's fate on the blank piece of paper.

Many variations may be seen in the way tonsure ceremony is performed. In most Hindu families, the priest is consulted. Generally, Monday is considered auspicious. On this day, the baby's *bua* or *phuphu* (paternal aunt) sits with it in her lap and the barber shaves the head. At the back of the crown a tuff of hair is left as *shikha*, commonly called *chundi*, which is the symbol of being a Hindu. However, I have observed that many consider keeping *shikha* as religious conservatism and backwardness. The *bua* is given gifts in cash or kind as *nega* according to one's pleasure and capacity. Feast is arranged on this day. Some have even gone to some sacred place on mainland for this ceremony.

Among Mopala Muslims, this is done on the seventh or fourteenth day at the mother's place when both the parties are invited for feast. The baby's father brings a goat or hen from his house. As soon as *ossan* (the barber) or *ossati* (female barber) touches the baby's head with razor, the *namazi* kills the goat or hen. The shaven hair is collected on a banana leaf and weighed in gold whose value in cash is distributed among family folks. The *ossan/ossati* is gifted rice, coconut, betelnut, betel leaves and clothes according to one's capacity. Among other Muslims, tonsure is done on the 40th day, when celebration is not necessary.

Annaprashan (First Cereal for Baby)

This ceremony, as in mainland India, is known here among Christian and Hindus as *kheer chatai* (licking *kheer*). This is done among Christians in the seventh month by the baby's elder *mama* (maternal uncle). *Kheer* is made of milk, rice and sugar.

In the absence of the elder *mama* some other relative may do it. In the past, *kheer* would be put in a *phool* (an alloy) vessel, which has been now been replaced by stainless steel.

Among Hindus, this ceremony is performed in the third, fifth, seventh or ninth month. Telegu-speaking Hindus and some other traditional families consider the fifth month as most auspicious for male and seventh or eighth month for female baby. An auspicious day is fixed in consultation with the priest, when the baby's *mama* brings a set of *thali*, tumbler, *katori* and spoon with which ceremony is performed. Later, these utensils are gifted for baby's use. If the *mama* is unemployed, these things are given by his parents. For this ceremony, a gold ring, or a gold or silver coin instead of a spoon, may be used. On this day, relatives and friends are invited and feasted.

In some Hindu families on this day, goods like toys, pen, paper, books, ink-pot, paper-knife, etc., are ceremoniously presented to the child. After *annaprashan* the baby is put in the room where all these items are displayed. There is a belief that the baby's future vocation will be related to the object that the baby touches. For example, its touching a book would mean teaching profession, or its touching a tool would imply engineering, and so on. Mopala Muslims do not have this ceremony; they may give cereals to the baby on any auspicious day.

Vidyaramba, Akshar Abhyas (Beginning of Education)

Generally, no ritual is observed when the child begins learning except among some orthodox Hindu families. Some Hindus on an auspicious day prescribed by the priest take the child to a temple where he makes an offering to the deity and then he is sent to school. Some other rituals are also observed in traditional Hindu families. Mr. A is a Telgu-speaking Hindu in whose family the child goes to school when he/she is five years old. On an auspicious day given by the priest or after consulting ephimaries, rice is spread in a thali and the child's fingers are moved to write *Om Namah Shivaya* (Hail Lord Shiva) and then the same *mantra* on a slate. On this day, small children and the teacher are invited. The invited children are presented sweets and slate-pencils. After the ceremony, the child is led to the school, for the first time.

Muslim children begin learning 'bismillah', in the *madarsa* as in mainland India. The boys start going to the *madarsa* when they are about five years of age. There they are taught the Koran and other religious teachings by a *maulavi*. On the first day in the *madarsa*, the child brings sweets, etc.

Ear-Piercing

This is done only to girls and no celebration takes place in any religious community on the occasion. Among Muslim, this ceremony comes under *sunnat*. Mopala Muslims call it *kad kusua* done to a girl above five. Before this *maulavi* or some knowledgeable recite *fatiha*. Piercing is done by *ossati*, female barber. On the occasion, it is recalled that the sea is calm, neither in low nor high tide, in the belief that there would be little bleeding.

Khatana (Circumcision Among Muslims)

It is practiced here also. The tip of the prepuce is cut. Traditionally, it is a very important ritual, also called *musalmani*. It is generally performed between the ages of three to ten-eleven years. Two flat, round-edged, absolutely smooth bamboo strips are inserted into the prepuce so that its snout envelops the strips, while *koran ayats* (verses) are being recited, the barber cuts the skin slowly. Mopala Muslims call it *sunnat-khatana* and is treated as first marriage. While performing it, special care is taken that the sea is in no low tide in the belief that there would be less bleeding. At present, it is performed by the private doctors or compounders. Some modern families even ignore this ritual. It is an occasion for celebration when close relatives bring several nourishing eatables for the child. *Khatana* is not performed on Friday.

Puberty-Menarche

The menarche ceremony indicative of coming of age called *sadana* in Tamil and *pedamasi* in Telagu, is generally not observed here even among South Indian families. It appears that now, under influence of new South Indian emigrants, it is picking up. In South India, women apply turmeric on the face and body during the periods which is not common in Andaman, but it can be seen being practiced increasingly under influence of new emigrants.

Marriage Rituals

Here, we describe in brief, the marriage rituals of different religions. Among Hindus, the bride's party goes to the bride-groom for *tilak*. From inside the house to *mandap* the boy's mother, who should not be a widow, brings the boy pouring water from *lota*. When the boy is seated, the priest of the girls' side performs rituals. Before applying *tilak* mark on the forehead, the mother covers the boy's head with her *pallav*, (end of saree). The *sala*, bride's brother, puts *tilak* and the two feed each other *pan batasha*. The barber of the girl's party tells people loudly about the items brought for the boy. Then comes the feast.

After *tilak, tel haldi* is performed. Mother, boy's sisters and other *suhagins* (women with living husband) go to a well. Brass pitcher is filled with water and covered by mango leaves and yellow cloth, coconut and betel nuts. The sister carries it on her head and brings it to *mandap* where she is presented *nega*, cloth, ornament, cash. Five *suhangins* putting water in the *lota* (pitcher) kept in the centre of the *mandap* and the mother having betel leaf, betel nut, etc., brings the boy from inside pouring water from *lota*. The boy is seated on the *mandap* and mother covers his head with *pallav*. Then five times each *tel-haldi* (mustard oil and turmeric) is touched on the head, shoulders, knees, and feet by five *suhagins*, which completes the ritual.

Then comes worshipping of the well. After bath, the boy is made to wear *sehara*. While the boy is standing, his mother performs his *arati* with seven flames and the seven wicks are thrown in seven directions. Then mothers sits putting *lota* in front. The boy circumabulates seven times. Mother stands up and blesses the son who says "I go to bring *bahu* for your service".

When *barat*, marriage party, reaches the girl's place young girls, bride's sisters, come to the boy with pitchers of water covered with coconut. Boy's party present them *nega* (cash). Bride's brother, *sala* brings *sharbat* (cold drinks) for the boy to drink. He is also given *nega*. The girl's mother performs *arati* and repeats what his mother has done. Then the boy is taken out holding hands from car by *sala* (brother-in-law). The girl's father receives the boy. Boy's mother does not come in *barat*. After recitation of *mantras* he is taken to *mandap* by *sala* either in lap or with hand on the back of the head and seats him there. A new practice has begun of late, that of *jayamal,* exchanging of garlands by bride and bridegroom.

For *saptapadi* (literally seven steps: seven perambulations with the bride around the sacrificial fire) the bride is seated in *mandap*. As the boy is brought by mother in his house pouring water so is the bride brought to *mandap* by her mother. The bride is veiled and dressed in full make-up with ornaments and gorgeous clothes and is seated beside the boy. After several rituals the bride and the bridegroom perambulate seven times around the sacrificial fire. Then curd in a small vessel is given to the bride and she makes the groom lick it seven times with a silver coin or gold ring and so does the groom.

Generally, at the time of *'gaudan'* (cow-gifting ceremony), a cow is not given. In the absence of the cow on the spot the formality is completed by *sankalpa* (deciding to do something). After several ritual the same night farewell preparation of *barat* begins. After the wedding, the boy's mother, who has not accompanied *barat*, comes to take the bride. *Saree* and ornaments given by boy's party is worn by the bride. The bride's mother leads pouring water from *lota* followed by the newly wed couple and others. *Barat* goes back in cars, scooters etc. as it had come. Sometimes, the bride's younger sister or some child of the family goes with her.

When *barat* reaches the boy's place his mother receives the couple and performs their *arati* with seven earthen lamps and then throws the lamps away from above their head in seven directions. Then, she leads pouring water from *lota* followed by the couple and other family folks. On the main entrance of the house, the couple are halted, by groom's sister to receive *nega* in cash or kind. Here too, the bride and the groom offers curd to each other. Then comes 'playful tricks' game in the form of picking a ring from a *thal* filled with water, etc. It is believed that whosoever wins would dominate in marital life in future.

As mentioned in the chapter on marriage, first visit of the bride after marriage to her parents is called *chauthi,* which falls on fourth day, though not observed necessarily. If the day is auspicious and convenient the couple goes otherwise some other auspicious day is fixed. For taking the bride, her parents, sisters, *bhabi* (brother's wife), etc. come. The groom's close relatives and friends stay there overnight. The next day, boy's mother and other relatives come to take her and groom. With this the cycle of marriage rituals is complete.

Tradition of cleaning *mandap* with cow dung is still prevalent. The same priest represents both the parties who conduct all marriage rituals but barbers may be two. As in the traditional Hindu marriages in the mainland here, the barber's role is not important in marriage ceremony. The wedding ceremony takes two to three hours.

Mopala Muslim marriage is similar to Hindu's like *nikah* on the day *barat* arrives, return of *barat* same night with bride, and *Chouthi* etc.

On the wedding day, three or four men of girl's house go to the boy's place to take *barat* called *tediveral* or *tedal*. They eat at the boy's place. On invited time, people gather at the boy's place. After snacks or feast in evening *barat* prepares to leave. The boy is clothed and decorated by folks coming from the girl's house. The wedding clothes are generally given by the groom's *jija*, sister's husband, which include *lungi*, longshirt, cap, shoes, etc. Now pants have replaced *lungi*. All sisters garland the boy and give him money. The boy seeks blessings from parents, relatives, and acquaintances. At the time of departure, according to Islamic tradition, the boy's mother cries. The boy's sister and other female relatives also go in *barat*. Song and dance in *barat* is Hindu influence. The *barat* is received at girl's place by seniors of the house. When the boy enters the bride's house it is customary that the bride's brother washes his hand and feet but now this is almost extinct. Now merely touching water vessel completes the formality. The *sala* holding water vessel is given *nega*. Then all male members sit in *mandap* and females go inside the house. The guests are offered *sharbat*, betel and cigarettes, etc. On maulavis (who is performing the *nikah*), asking, two elders of the house go to the bride and say in Mopala Malayali, "your *nikah* is to take place with so and so. Do you accept?" Her silence is considered acceptance or she may speak so. Maulavi recites *nikah* and the bride's father holding the boy's hand says, "I am marrying my daughter with you for this *mehar* amount (generally Rs 101 or more or less according to one's status and capacity). On maulvi's direction the boy says, "I accept the offered girl as *nikah* in lieu of the said *mehar* amount". Then the amount is paid in cash to the bride's father. The boy is given some money, Rs 51 to 501, by the girl's party, which is called *keting gijje* (or *tilak*). After reading *nikah,* maulavi reads prayer. The boy offers salutation to the girl's father and then begins the feast after which the *barat* with the boy returns without bride. The family girls coming in *barat* and one or two males stay back who decorate the bride and take her to the groom's house with her parents and other family women. Though Mopala Muslims have no *purda* system yet the bride's head is covered. As they come close to the boy's place there is song and music. Both the parties question answer through songs. Some senior females of the boy's family invite bride and women in. Bride's feet is washed by her *nanad*, husband's sister and receives *nega*. Then bride's parents after handing her over to the boy's parents take leave with others.

Chouthi takes place generally after a week. The bride's younger brother along with others goes to fetch the couple. In the evening the couple with the boy's friends go to the bride's place and staying overnight return by next noon. On this occasion, bantering and joking are done with the boy's party. There is a difference in Mopala Muslim marriage rituals and that of other Muslims. When the *barat* reaches bride's house the boy is carried to *mandap* in the lap of girl's brother or of some other family member. Unlike Mopala's, there is no custom of pouring water on the feet. At the time of *nikah* two seniors take the girl's consent. The boy comes wearing the *seharas,* one of which he gives for the bride. After *nikah* and feast the bride goes with the groom; not like Mopalas in whom the bride goes separately with party. Sometimes, only a child goes. *Chouthi* ceremony may take place on the fourth day or any succeeding day. But it is not fixed when they will return, some people return the same day some two days later. Now people have lunch at bride's place, see a film in the evening and go back to the boy's place from there.

All Christians also observe *chouthi.* Since Christian marriage is performed in the Church, therefore, to a great extent marriage rituals are similar.

Death Rites

Death rites differ from one religion to another. It is to be noted that rites that had become extinct or modified according to circumstances have revived again because of the coming of new emigrants and interactive relationship established with mainland India.

The Hindus call a priest at a person's death and the priest looks into the planetary position (*grah dasha*). If death has occurred under *panchak* planetary position small images made of flour and other material with bean seed eyes is put on seven places for liberation. The corpse is bathed and then putting it on bamboo scaffolding with coconut leaf mat they take it to *murdakhadi*, bay of the dead, at *Jungalighat*. Close relatives go in funeral procession; women do not go in the procession. At every crossing on the way a family member, breaks a coconut. The eldest son gives first shoulder to the body and performs the death rites.

If the dead is a woman with living husband, a *suhagin*, her shroud is red or pink. In case of widow and male it is white. Small children, unmarried persons, pregnant women and unmarried girls are not burnt but buried. The body is never immersed in the sea. If a person when alive has asked for certain rite to be performed, it is performed to honour his wish.

For three days kitchen fire is not lit. Food comes from relatives or neighbours. He who lits the pyre has to eat saltless food for three days. Most eat rice or chapati with milk. For a year after death no festival is celebrated by the family. On the eleventh day after death, son's head is shaven at a well or pond away from house. A lock of hair, *shikha* is left while shaving. These days in the event of death of some close relative, adults do not go in for shaving their head; instead family children are shaven. On the eleventh day, *ekadashah*, people are invited for food. When a woman dies, the first community feeding is on ninth day and second on eleventh day. One year after death another community feeding is arranged as *shraaddh*. The cot and some clothes of the dead are given to the barber along with new clothes in the name of the dead.

A Christian's corpse is carried in a wooden coffin. The church priest is informed. The artisan (generally close friend or relative) is asked to make the coffin in a short time whose cost is generally not taken. The cloth fixed on the outer coffin differs according to marital status of the dead. In case of a married person, outer cloth is black and inner white but in case of an unmarried person both are white. The coffin lid has a cross sign of some bright cloth. Women do not go in the burial procession. Men carry the coffin on their shoulders to the graveyard, where the coffin is kept in a room at the gate and is taken in when the priest comes. There the priest prays and family members lower the coffin into the grave. After prayer, the priest throws a handful of earth on the coffin followed by all who have come with the body. Finally, some family members fill in the pit completely.

The family of the dead invite friends and relatives on the third day after death. Some offer *kheer*. On that day, family members go to the grave and pour milk on it and burn candle and josstick which is repeated on fortieth day also. Every year candle and josstick are lit. All souls day is celebrated on second November when in the evening four members of the family of the dead and the church priest go to the graveyard to pray and light candle and josstick. People maintain the grave. An earthen grave is given new layer of clay.

Death rites of Mopala and other Muslims are much similar to those of mainland India. As in mainland India, after the death of a man, the wife does not see the face of the dead husband instead she holding his feet asks for his forgiveness for all that she has done. The body is laid straight, covered with a white sheet with face towards the south. The body is bathed before burial. The coffin is brought from mosque. Mopalas carry the coffin to the mosque and there recite *mazzatenishkaram*. Other Muslims recite religious verses concerning death. When putting the body in the coffin, it is covered with new white cloth. The shroud is 22 metres long for adults and 13 metres for minors. The dead person's ears, mouth and palm are filled with cotton. Wailing for the dead is prohibited by religion. Death procession is led by a person who recites *jikar,* which is repeated by others following the coffin. Only men go in the funeral procession, with heads covered.

The sexton who digs grave is a Muslim. After reciting *jikar* the body is lowered into the grave with face open but rest of the body covered. The body is laid supine with face turned towards the south. Though *purda* system is not practised in early emigrant Muslim community of Andaman, but the old custom can be seen in the burial when female dead are put in *purda*. The body is lowered into grave after reciting *jikar* and is covered with a wooden plank costing Rs 4. Then *fatiha* is read. After a close relative has thrown a handful of soil, all blood relatives do the same. Then it is fully covered with soil. After going seven steps, nobody looks back at the grave.

On the day of death, a *maulavi* is called who reads *fatiha* in the house. Third day, he is called again to do so and is fed. On this day, food is distributed to children in the mosque. On the seventh day, maulavi is called again to read *fatiha*. On the fortieth day, a large-scale community feast is held like *trayodashah*, (corrupt form *terahi,* of Hindus), in which *kheer* is an essential item. A year later, another community feast is arranged according to one's capacity. The 40th day feast is important before which nothing important is done.

Though on every Friday, there is a custom for close relatives to go to the grave to read *fatiha* after *Jumma namaz* yet it is followed only by few Muslims. It is believed that on this day the dead parents sit on the grave. Some arrange koran recitation for the dead parents for forty days. Many other mainland religious practices are also found here.

Generally, Hindus believe that if some relative or another Hindu has died, then for thirteen days, there should be no celebrations, song or dance in the locality. This applies for ten days in case of the death of member of some other religious community.

Fasting

Early emigrant Hindu women observe fast on different auspicious occasions. Males comparatively observe fewer fasts. As in mainland India, women here have deep faith in keeping fast on *Shivaratree*, *Janmashtami* and other weekdays. On fast days certain rules are observed, for example, on Fridays, women and girls observing *Santoshi Mata* fast, worship and offer jaggery and parched gram after morning bath. On this day, no sour food item is used and only *phalahar* (literally fruits but in practice certain prescribed eatables) is taken. Simple meal is taken only once in a day, at night. The Monday fast is that of Lord Shiva in which after morning bath the woman goes to a *peepal* tree to worship and lights an earthen lamp beneath the tree. Fasting throughout the day, she eats sweet *chapati* at night.

Fast is observed for different purposes, in which concerned prohibitions on the direction of priests are observed. There are religious women who believe that by not observing a fast strictly, there can be serious repercussions. Here is an instance: A 25 years old unmarried Hindu woman 'A' died after falling from a scooter. Miss 'B' 32, an unmarried primary school teacher says in this connection that she dreamt one night that she had killed a serpent and covered it with a white cloth. Since a snake is a symbol of Shiva so killing it is inauspicious. Comparing white cloth with the winding sheet, she connected the dream with an event that 'A' observed Monday fast of Shiva and would light an earthen lamp beneath a *peepal* tree. After observing fast for sixteen Mondays she lit the lamp in the house instead of beneath the *peepal* tree, completing the ritual which should not be done because Lord Shiva may get angry or pleased in no time. Since the fast was not observed properly so, as a result of incurring Shiva's anger, 'A' died in an ordinary scooter accident.

Traditional religious bindings are comparatively less in social life of early emigrants, for example, in matters of regularity in going to the temple, mosque, or church, generally Hindus would go to the temple on some religious occasion or just casually. Hindu women are more religious than men. There are few Muslims who read *namaz* five times a day. Christians also go to church occasionally. Like visit to religious places, worship in the house is also less frequent. People do not have faith in godman. This does not mean that these are more of 'rationalism' among the people. Rather most believe seriously in different superstitions of magic-totem.

Superstitions

A large amount of facts were gathered on this aspect during the study. We describe here some superstitions observed by many people:

1. As in mainland India, Hindus believe that before going out on an auspicious mission eating curd and sugar ensures success.
2. If one suffers from frequent boils, a piece of paper and pen is taken from his hand on which names of three usurers are written and then tied on the sufferer's arm. His suffering would end within three days and the usurers would have boils.
3. If poultry farm hens fall sick and die then as soon a hen dies it should be hung upside down and circling it seven times at the poultry farm gate one should throw it from above. This will cure other hens.
4. If neighbouring houses are on fire and fire is spreading towards one's house then one should throw curd up in front of the house and the house will remain unaffected.
5. If one desires a female baby one should give in one's wife's hand a piece of paper on which Parvati is written. Then only a daughter will be born.

6. If one always loses in gambling, one should keep in his pocket a small piece of noose of rope with which a person has committed suicide. He will always win.

Besides, people believe in different types of magic and totem. People from Chota Nagpur of Bihar, locally known as Ranchi, and Bengali refugees and emigrants are considered experts in black magic. Among early emigrants, Mopalas are comparatively less superstitious. It is said that the *shamans* dig out the first dead baby and perform different acts of black magic. Some use post-delivery entrail snatched away from a black cat for magical rites.

Some important superstitions are described below, which are believed to be realised through some black magic art. To attain the desired beloved, some hair from her head is procured with which a squirrel is tied and then buried. After some days, the hair is taken out, treated with some *mantra* and then kept in the girl's way so that she crosses over it. And then the girl becoming infatuated will come to the boy's house on her own. A person's name is muttered while writing it on a piece of paper and treated with *mantra*. The paper is then tied to a frog's mouth and as it dilates so would concerned person's stomach, leading to his death after a while. If an enemy is to be killed then *shaman* will shoot a magic arrow at a tree. The arrow pierces the tree and as the tree withers the concerned person will waste and die in a few days.

Belief in Spirits

Besides magic-totem, people believe in spirits commonly known as *hawa* (air) or devil. It is heard that so and so is possessed by *hawa* or so and so is afflicted by *hawa* or devil. It is believed that during Japanese occupation many met with untimely death and their thirsty spirits are wandering – though even before this event people believed in it. Practitioners in *tantra* and demonology (like *Ojha* in the mainland) employed to pacify or tame evil spirits, charge Rs 50-200. It is believed that the possessed ask for certain things like sacrifice of goat or hen. The *shamans* do not pay heed to it and try to exorcise the spirit through *mantras* and others devices. Some put their mouth on different body parts to catch *hawa* and it is believed that they capture and shut it in a bottle, which is then buried on his direction. It is said that the possessed loses appetite.

Methods to exorcise spirits are same in all religions; like wearing talisman, reciting *mantra*s (*jhad-phoohk*), or sacrificing the demanded animal. The *shaman* should be given whatever he asks for or he would let loose *hawa*. Here is an anecdote. "One day a Ranchi shaman after exorcising the *hawa,* passed through his friend's house and asked for a hen to eat. The friend had a hen but being poor didn't offer it to him. The angry shaman attacked him with 'spirit'. Within hours his wife started gibbering. The shaman was requested to help but he refused saying he won't treat one who could not feed him a hen. Even now the woman would gibber and at odd times go to jungle and sit on her child's grave."

Here is another anecdote narrated by 'A', a Brahmin: "Many years ago, when I was a class X student in the month of December *Satya-narain Katha* (a religious function in which lord's story is narrated) was arranged. My elder sister had come from her in-law's place and stayed overnight. While returning at night, she felt upset and it was found that she was possessed. A *shaman* was called who said she was afflicted by devil. After reading of *mantra*s, it was found that the evil spirit possessing her is that of a man who was killed some years ago by the Burmese and thrown into a well at Lambaline. A month ago, when she was passing that way, the evil spirit of 'Mewalal' entered her. When called, the spirit said it would go away if a hen is sacrificed. The *shaman* did not agree because sometimes spirits cheat and demand bigger things. For three days, he interrogated the woman who would forget her answers when in senses. Every time, when questioned, the spirit would say, 'liberate me I have no family members. I am Mewalal. Burmese had thrown me in the well after killing me.' He would also tell the causes of murder. When many known witch craft experts failed, a Bengali Muslim was called. As soon as he reached near the house, my sister who was in the kitchen fainted. She was laid in another room. As the *shaman* reached the door even before seeing him she shouted, 'You rotten Bengali, you have come again!' The man kept mum and asked for different things. Coming beside my sister, he began his *mantra*. When the spirit did not leave, he gave fumes of black pepper, and threatened, 'you wicked if you do not leave I would put you in bottle and throw you in sea.' This worked and then the spirit left saying, it would never come again. As it left, my sister shivered violently and her body became absolutely cold. Since then she is all right."

There are many other incidents of spirits of murder or suicide victims possessing someone or more persons. I found that the most of the victims are females. A Sunni Muslim working as a senior clerk said that one day a spirit strangulated him. The spirit (*shaitan*, devil) would sit on a tree in front. Just when he was about to die, somehow the spirit released him. He said, "Whenever the spirit comes there is a peculiar smell."

It is generally believed that on some specific spots invisible 'devil' or spirits live such as Diganabad, near Babuline well or Vijaybagh gate, etc. Generally, all early emigrants are afraid of ghosts, spirits and the like.

To keep family protected from evil spirits, Mopalas and other Muslims hang Koran *ayats* inscribed on copper plates. Hindus nail horseshoe on entrance and other parts of the house. Hindus and others do not bother about direction of entrance for the house. But at foundation laying ceremony Hindu, Muslim, and Christians call the priest. Besides foundation laying, when stairs are constructed *pooja* is performed by masons only. House-warming ceremony (*Grih Pravesh*) is observed as in mainland. Christians take new scooter or motorcycle to church priest who, reading blessing from Bible, sprinkles holy water on the owner of vehicle and on the machine. The above description shows that early emigrants are pretty superstitious.

Festivals

Almost all major festivals are celebrated. There is no specific festival of local origin. All festivals have the same form externally as on mainland but there are internal changes. Durgapuja, Deepavali, Holi, Rakshabandhan, Shivaratri, Janmashtami are major Hindu festivals. Id, Bakerid among Muslims and Christmas among Christians. Deepavali, Holi and Rakshabandhan are celebrated by followers of other religions also. *Durgapuja* and *Saraswati puja* committees also have Christian and Muslim members. Bhaiyaduj is not celebrated. All Muslims mourn during Muharram but only few *tazias* are brought out by Shias, that too after the coming of new Shia emigrants. On Makar Sankranti, Hindu families go to 'Carvins cove beach' for bath and cooking and eating. Most people participate in festival of other religions. With large number of new emigrants many festivals are now celebrated on a much larger scale.

To conclude, we may say that externally, there is a lot of similarity between mainland rituals and belief and that of early emigrants in Andaman. However, internally according to circumstances and necessity, modifications have come. Most close persons take part in rituals and religious occasions.

Note

1. Shah, P.G., *The Dublas of Gujarat*, Bhartiya Adimjati Sevak Sangh, Kingsway, Delhi, May 1958.

8 Conclusion and Generalisation

In this chapter, we present the main conclusions based on the factual materials spread over seven chapters of this study about continuity and change in an emigrant society. Since Hindus pre-dominated the early emigrant society and so also the bulk of the sample households for this study, the contextualisation of many of the observations has to follow this frame of reference.

Historical Growth of Andaman as a Penal Settlement

The British by using the Andaman Islands as the notorious *Kala Pani* from 1858, that is, soon after the collapse of the first war of Indian Independence, brought them to the notice of international politics. In March 1942 during World War II, the Islands were occupied by the Japanese, but they came again under British control in October 1945, and soon after its status as a penal settlement ended.

The prisoners sent here were clearly categorised into two sets: political and criminal. Prisoners of either category were encouraged to settle here after completing their sentence. Indeed, women prisoners, even those convicted for relatively lesser crimes, were specially requisitioned from the mainland. It is important to mention here that though thousands of political prisoners were deported here, they mostly returned home on release.

At the close of the penal settlement and its passage into a 'free' territory, it was, thus, mostly the dangerous criminals or their progeny that remained. This fact is also corroborated by the respondents to this study, as 74.7 per cent of them reported that their predecessors were exiled here for heinous crime like dacoity, murder, etc., and settled here on release. The selection was only natural. The political prisoners had all the reasons to return, and the criminals to hold back, specially when they had already taken some roots here as 'self-supporting prisoners'. With the settlement of prisoners, also came government servants, traders and labourers some of whom decided to settle here for various reasons: availability of land allotments being the foremost. All of them formed a 'new society' under most adverse circumstances. There was a larger influx in the later years specially as a large number of 'refugees' arrived in the wake of partition of the country, and a new 'dividing line' was drawn. Thus, predecessors and those who had originally arrived here before 1947 are called 'early emigrants' (or 'local born'), and those who followed became 'new emigrants'. As the pressure on the resources and employment opportunities in the government sector increased, the dividing line became sharper. The present study is based on early emigrants of the capital town, Port Blair where they have a much bigger presence. From the point of the special focus of the study, the early emigrants were regarded as more relevant and fascinating, for their first generation was forcibly and completely cut off from their social moorings and their off-springs scarcely had any contact with their roots. So, the social and cultural patterns that evolved were more or less 'mixed'.

Contact Language

In early years of penal settlement, people of different religions, provinces and linguistic regions were brought here, and no linguistic group was socially viable to mainly communicate within itself. A purely hybrid kind of Hindi was born which has been known here as Hindustani, and it is used at home by 82.2 per cent of early emigrants. The researcher's own experiences during field work shows that the language is not only gender-neutral, it follows even in the written form, hardly any rules of grammar. The general census however, does not recognise any of these divisions between 'early' and 'new' emigrants or administrative, linguistic, cultural regions of origin. There is no demographic or socio-economic data available on these important aspects.

At present, early and new emigrants of different religions and provinces are living in Port Blair town. Among early emigrants, Hindus are in majority with 56.8 per cent, followed by Muslims, Christians and Sikhs in that order. Most of them hail from Uttar Pradesh (23.6%), Kerala, West Bengal and the erstwhile Madras province. There are also other people and people of tribal origins, such as Mopala, Bhantu, Ranchi, the Chhota Nagpur tribal fragments, who because of their dress and other cultural characteristics have their separate identity. During penal settlement period the Ranchi people were brought here in groups, mostly as labour for forest felling and land reclamation. They also settled in clusters. In this way they were able to maintain a regional-cultural identity, though there has been quite some inter-mixing as the others merged into these major groups. All these groups and people are known in local society by their original regional/ethnic names.

Pattern of Early Emigrant Settlement

British officers' policy was not to settle an ethnic or regional-cultural group in one place for administrative reasons. With a view to also bringing more land under cultivation, they were scattered over a large area. As the population increased and new families were raised, a process of clustering of the ethnically linguistically or regionally similar population also started, giving rise to a discernible neighbourhood pattern. In recent years because of allotment of residential plots by the administration on random basis, people with diverse regional-cultural characteristics (by origin) have settled in mixed colony in a specific area. However, the village settlement in south Andamans resembles the villages on mainland India. For example, there is concentration of population of Bhantus in Katelganj area and of Mopalas in Weembarliganj.

Continuity and Indistinct Form of Caste System

The Hindu prisoners exiled to the penal settlement came from a society in which caste system was an important element. British officers had full knowledge of nature and characteristics of caste system and its use from the point of political control. Hence, they took full cognisance of caste consciousness of prisoners. The administrators were particularly cautious not to offend caste feelings in work allotment. All 'unclean' or degrading work was allotted to members of untouchable caste only, to the extent that if sufficient hands were not available among the prisoners for unclean work, like scavenging, prisoners of specific caste would be requisitioned from mainland. There was however, a limited possibility of caste system reasserting itself here in its full form. From the time of penal settlement itself, there are instances of low caste people claiming to be and behaving like high caste. The 1908 Gazetteer and census reports of that period mention that the Hindus in the settlement were divided into Brahmin, Kshatriya, Vaishya and Shudra categories. But apparently for reasons of lack of demographic viability of some caste categories and want of any occupational differentiation the Hindu population came to be divided in two broad caste divisions: high caste (*savarna*) and low caste (*avarna*). Under the former came Brahmin, Kshatriya, Vaishya and the remaining under the latter. During voyage to the island and under extremely hard conditions in the penal settlement, observance of caste-based prohibitions of food, water and untouchability was not possible, yet conservative Hindus observed them to the extent it was practicable. The low caste exile particularly having been transported beyond the traditional spatial boundaries and the shackles of the caste structure, used this situation to abandon caste-based norms of behaviour and caste identity. Its effect is seen even now. No less than 38.5 per cent of respondents in this study did not mention their castes. Because of this, many scholars have inferred that there is no caste system in Andaman. But the reality is something different. Evidently the Hindus are generally conscious of the caste system, though they may not use the caste labels. Generally, the parents inform their children about the caste background of the other families in their neighbourhood, and to quite some extent their social interaction is influenced by it.

Unlike the Britishers, the Japanese occupation army hardly paid any heed to caste affiliations in work allotment or residential arrangements. Their forced intervention did contribute to a virtual breakdown of the system. On the contrary, the large influx of new emigrants after independence has tended to reconstruct the caste system. Among the early emigrants, the general tendency is that those who consider it worth showing off in term of social status, reveal their caste and those who do not, would not do it. So, it cannot be said that the early emigrant is a 'casteless' society but it is not certainly regulated by caste in any rigid manner.

As in mainland India, among early Muslim and Christian emigrants, we find signs of parallel caste system. During early days of the penal settlement, we find instances of religious conversion in the hope of better access and social position but such converts are looked down upon by others. Muslims like Pathan and Sheikh, consider themselves superior to rest of Muslims such as the majority Mopalas. The same applies to Christians, also. A Kshatriya or Vaisya convert Christian considers himself superior to low caste converts. However, the caste status plays very little role in determining one's social status, especially in the urban segment. Since, most of the heads of households are in government service, it is the position in the bureaucratic hierarchy that matters.

Family and Marital Life

The actual transformation of this penal settlement was based on permission to prisoners to lead a family life for which they were allowed to call their families from India, or to marry female prisoners here subject to fulfilment of certain conditions. Some families did come from India but the Hindus especially were dissuaded from calling them for fear of social boycott. There were far too fewer women as compared to men in the settlement, despite the prison authorities specially requisitioning deportation of more female prisoners from the mainland. As a result, there were all sorts of sexual aberrations and crimes against women, many of whom were virtually forced into prostitution. As one of the consequences, under such circumstances, the traditional sort of marital ties were hardly possible and evidently a great deal of normlessness pervaded in that period.

On the positive side, some old members of the community feel that the great scarcity of women in early times affected their social position. Women were highly regarded for this reason and they continue to have a say not only in family matters but also participation in economic activities also.

Scarcity of women had widely affected the institution of marriage. Among Hindus, observance of rules of exogamy and endogamy was not feasible. Since Hindus were reduced to only two broad social divisions, high and low castes. The general tendency was marriages taking place within these two broad divisions. Though there are few instances of marriage between high and low caste but it is only between high caste male and low caste female which is in a way a counter-establishment of principles of mixed marriage, *anulom vivah*. Generally, mother's caste is given no importance. Thus, partially inter-caste marriage tradition began more as a compromise to the situation, but the effort was always to at least, stick to whatever was practicable.

Scarcity of women had some other positive effects, like absence of problem of widow remarriage, and dowry. Child marriage was restrained by the government at one stage. But it has not revived. At the most such cases must be rare. There are other customs, which were abolished in one stroke under force, but there was no reaction even when force was removed. For instance, when Japanese occupied the islands, they banned Hindu women wearing veil or Muslim women wearing *burqua* lest these provided cover for spying against them. And even today, unlike in mainland India, we do not see veil or *burqua*.

Nearly half the families (47.1%) are nuclear and remaining intermediate, joint or single, etc. The main reason for the emergence of nuclear family is the absence of joint productive activity like trade or agriculture and also owing to the dependence on service, occupations. Likewise, even in the joint families its more a 'contributory' system, that is, members do not hand over their total income to the head of the family, but contribute a definite sum every month to the family kitty, retaining the rest as personal income. Like in mainland India, generally the senior most male member is head of the family.

Average size of family is 6.8 with 3.3 females and 3.5 males. Obviously, the sex ratio is balanced at the point, as our sample population show 926 female for every 1,000 males. This is contrary to the very adverse sex ratio presented in the census of the total population. Age-wise average number of members per family is: 20-54 years 2.9 and 3.2 members are children or old people. Comparatively, there are more children and old persons than the active or earning member on whom they are dependent.

The institution of marriage is as universal here as anywhere in the country, the age of marriage both for boys and girls is somewhat higher across all social groups, relative to the mainland society. The family system appears to be quite stable. The incidence of divorce or legal separation, or desertion is negligible, though the differential between widows (3.9%) and widowers (1%) in almost equal size of population must raise a few questions. It is reported that even the problem of dowry is shooting up. This may not auger well for the women's status in the 'early emigrant' community which it seems had come to value women for their relative 'scarcity' in their midst.

The process of match making for marriage is a curious mixture of 'love' and 'arranged' marriages not unknown in the urban society in the mainland also. But, probably it is more prevalent here. The proportion of inter-religious, inter-community, inter-caste (even as a broad cluster) 'love' or 'love-cum-arrange' marriages must be many times more here, and these are socially accepted, may be after some initial hitch in some cases.

The same sort of mixed attitude operates in the matter of adherence to traditional customs/rituals and modern attitudes. For example, the priest would be consulted for finding an auspicious day/time for a marriage ceremony and yet the client would indicate his convenience that it should be on a weekend or holiday. Similarly, the ceremonies/rituals may be curtailed according to convenience.

Monogamy is the most prevalent form of marriage even among the Muslims. Only some conservative Mopalas, more so in the rural segment go for more than one wife. Muslim and Christian marriage institutions are influenced by Hindu customs like Christian women putting vermilion in hair parting and Muslims using band and music in *barat* etc. Certainly Hindus are in majority, but the extension of their social customs and norms seems to be voluntary and there was no resentment expressed on this account.

Organisational Set-up

From the very beginning, early emigrants have been looked down with contempt and hate. The 1931 census report says, "Indian officers look them with hate because on the one hand they were descendants of prisoners and on the other they do not strictly observe traditional rules of caste and religion especially in matrimonial alliances." Local Born Association accepts only pre-1942 emigrants or descendants as members. It is a secular organisation and does not make any distinction on the basis of religion and caste; they have tried to overcome this prejudice by creating an identity and organising for assertion of their rights as a special category.

Economic and Occupational Life

In early period of penal settlement prisoners were put to unskilled work only. As penal settlement's requirements increased, they were allowed to take up various occupations but under tight administrative control. The prisoners attaining self-supporter status had agriculture as the main source of livelihood. During 1923-31, because of new employment opportunities in government offices, 50 per cent moved towards them. Easy availability of government jobs reduced the importance of agriculture. At present, most of the early emigrant families have government service as their main occupation. Inter-generation occupational mobility among early emigrants of Port Blair under the study indicates that whereas the occupation of grandfathers of 63.8 per cent respondents was agriculture, it was 27.2 per cent in their father's time and merely 0.6 per cent in the present generation. However, most of them are in middle or lower middle grade jobs. As in mainland India, in the beginning early emigrants were not in favour of women doing service. But gradually because of easy availability of jobs and demonstration effect of new emigrant women, especially Malayali women from early emigrant society are also coming forward for formal employment.

Though there are large numbers of families of low caste origin, but actually they have raised their status through spatial change by tearing-off from their native communities and traditional occupation.

The economic conditions of the early emigrant families are generally better-off. They have steady jobs in the government sector; generally there are more than one salaries coming to a family; there is no unemployment. Moreover, they derive certain advantages for being the early settlers; they have incomes from agricultural lands allotted to them in the early phase, as well as rental incomes.

In totality, average number of earning member per family is 2.19 with monthly income of Rs 1,423.38. This income analysis shows that each member of early emigrant society has monthly income of Rs 208.38. On the whole, there are 3.13 dependent persons per earning member. Looking at the distribution of expenditure, we find that considerable part of income goes to basic necessities like food and vegetables.

Though 17.34 per cent of early emigrant families are under average debt of Rs 2,042.19 yet significantly none has taken loan from any private source. Main reasons for taking loan are house building or repair, business, purchasing two-wheelers etc. All loans have been taken from respective departments or banks. Craving for material objects such as tendency to buy radio, two-wheelers, tape recorders, etc., seems to be increasing. Looking at houses, their interior decoration and reported family income, it can certainly be said that economic status of early emigrants is comparatively better.

Cultural Life

The different rituals, customs, religious practices and even superstitions externally appears the same, but internally they have got modified according to situations or convenience. In the beginning there were priests only from Uttar Pradesh, hence rituals of all Hindus were performed on UP pattern. Muslim and Christian rituals changed comparatively less yet many Hindu customs have entered theirs, and its pervasive influence is visible. We started with the hypothesis that if people with different socio-cultural characteristics, forcibly removed from their organic society and exiled, to another place, especially in conditions like in a 'penal settlement', the 'synthetic society' that is formed in the process, is bound to loose many of its cultural refinements and undergo a process of impoverishment. Certainly, the early emigrants or the island society for that matter have not created any innovative cultural pattern, be it in social values, art-like values or music. It resembles a rather crude form of synthesis, but it is certainly a interesting experiment in evolution of a multi-ethnic, multi-religious society.

In the spheres of socio-economic and political interaction, 'same caste identity' has become secondary. Division in Andaman is on the basis of year of emigration: pre- and post-independence are main dividers. Large influx of post-independence emigrants has turned the early emigrants into a minority. Though the islands have a large developmental potential, yet development is limited to the governmental sphere. Early emigrants see a threat to their existence and rights because of increasing population of new emigrants. Early emigrants have organised to claim preferential treatment in distribution of all jobs, and other economic opportunities. The administration has also provided job reservation for them. This has become a cause of tension between new and early emigrants. Ill-will between the two societies is clearly visible and there are instances of conflict. Early emigrant society is also dissatisfied with high officials in administration and other departments coming on deputation for a specific period from mainland. They demand educated and competent 'local born' to be appointed on these posts. So far as the rest of the society is concerned, new emigrants and various high officials look down upon these so-called descendants of prisoners. At the same time, they also seem to be scared of them. New emigrants and high officials have the tendency to maintain distance from early emigrants in socio-cultural and even political sphere.

The above concluding observations make it amply clear that the early emigrant society of Andaman is a sort of a synthetic society that developed in compulsive circumstances. In this society from the formative period, rapid changes came in institutions and behaviour. It may be noted that around the time of establishment of Andaman penal settlement, shiploads of 'indentured' labour from India were transported to British colonies in many parts of world, like Fiji, Mauritius, East Africa, British Guyana, Surinam, etc. It may be a proper subject of comparative study. But there were some vital differences between these two streams of migration; e.g., (a) the indentured labour were drafted in large number from particular regional society, (b) wherever, these labourers were taken they were settled in clusters, mostly in sugar plantations. As a result, these labour colonies developed into homogeneous communities. Besides, there also was a process of interaction with locals and labourers from other countries. But conditions in Andaman was different. First, except some groups like the Mopala, Chhota Nagpur tribals and Bhantu, a criminal tribe, from North India, individuals from different regions of India reached there as exiles. Secondly, because of small number of native tribals who lived in far off jungles, there was no opportunity for interaction. Therefore, emigrant community of Andaman remained in true sense, merely a counter-shadow of the mainland.

People exiled in groups had a kind of social interactivity. Hence, to a great extent for them creation of a transplanted society could be possible and because of which still they are able to maintain their identity. On the contrary, this was not possible for smaller fragments of population.

However, even among the early emigrants, it is mostly the urban dwellers who have better access to the employment opportunities and facilities. The people of tribal origin have remained backward. For example, Ranchi people originally transported from Chhota Nagpur to fell forests and reclaim land for agriculture, are still concentrated in the rural sector, as small cultivators or labourers. Similarly, Andaman Mopalas are still engaged in petty jobs, shopkeeping, fishing or agriculture. The settlement pattern too, has been a major factor in perpetuation of their condition, since initially they were settled in distinct clusters and put on manual jobs.

At present, among new emigrants the basis of social organisation and mobility is not mainly on caste or any other homogenous division. Homogenising and political functions of caste is very weak, especially among early emigrants. The solidarity of the group is more on the issue of their being the early settlers. And so are visible other processes of secularisation.

Here, it is important to mention that after the influx of new emigrants to the islands, we notice certain tendencies of reversal or retrogression of some progressive trends of social change. For example, certain social practices that downgrade the women's status, attempts at religious mobilisation, and signs of caste consciousness especially among those claiming higher caste origin.

In the end, our study proves that movement of population, even involuntary, is a strong factor of social change. Whatever be the factors (like socio-regional background of emigration, their numerical size, settlement pattern), the speed of change and qualitative aspects of change are also revealed by this study. Regarding forced emigration, it becomes a "forced model of change" but one differentiation is essential that if the exiles are kept for long under environment of repression, the boundaries of change are very small, and on the contrary if they get free environment, change is fast.

Bibliography

Books

Abrams, Charles, *Man's Struggle for Shelter in an Urbanizing World: An Adaptation*, Current Thought Series, No. 2, Vakils, Feffer and Nimsons Pvt. Ltd., 1964.

Ali, Hamid, *The Moplah, Malabar and its Folk*, edited by T.K. Gopal Panikkar, 3rd edn., Madras, G.A. Natesan and Company, 1929.

Altekar, A.S., *The Position of Women in Hindu Civilization*, Motilal Banarasi Das, Varanasi, 1956.

Andrew, E.J.L., *The Labour in Rangoon*, Oxford University Press, London, 1933.

Arasaratnam, S., *Indians in Malaysia and Singapore*, Oxford University Press, Kuala Lumpur, 1970.

Atal, Yogesh, *The Changing Frontiers of Caste*, National Publishing House, Delhi, 1968.

Aurora, G.S., *The New Frontiersmen: A Sociological Study of Indian Immigrants in the United Kingdom*, Bombay, Popular Prakashan, 1967.

Bagley, W.A., *Facts and How to Find Them*, Pitman Publishing Corporation, London, 1938.

Bailey, F.G., *Caste and the Economic Frontier*, University Press, Manchester, 1957.

Berreman, G.D., *Hindus of the Himalayas*, Berkeley and Los Angles, University of California Press, 1963.

Bhagwan Prasad, *Socio-Economic Study of the Urban Middle Classes*, Sterling Publishers Pvt. Ltd., Delhi, 1968.

Brown, A.R. Radcliffe, *Andaman Islands*, 'The Free Press of Glencoe', U.S.A., 1964.

— *Structure and Function in Primitive Society*, The English Language Book Society and Cohen and West Ltd., London, 1964.

Burrows, Raymond, *Indian Life and Labour in Natal*, Johannesburg: South African Institute of Race Relation, 1952.

Chak, B.L., *Green Island in the Sea*, Publication Division, Ministry of Information and Broadcasting, Government of India, Delhi, August 1967.

Chakravarti, N.R., *The Indian Minority in Burma: The Rise and Decline of an Immigrant Community*, Oxford University Press, 1971.

Cipriani, Lidio, *The Andaman Islanders*, Edited and Translated by D. Tayler Cox, Weidenfeild and Nicolson, London, 1966.

Desai, I.P., *Some Aspects of Family in Mahuva*, Asia Publishing House, Bombay, 1965.

Devanandan and Thomas, *The Changing Pattern of Family in India*, Christian Institute for the study of Religion and Society, Bangalore, 1960.

Dhasmana, M.M., *The Ramos of Arunachal*, Concept Publishing Co., New Delhi, 1979.

Dube, Leela, *Sociology of Kinship*, Popular Prakashan, Bombay, 1947.

Dube, S.C., *Indian Village*, Routledge and Kegan Paul, London, 1955.

Dubois, A.J.A., *Hindu Manners and Customs*, Clarendon Press, Oxford, 1899.

Dutta, P.C., *The Great Andamanese: Past and Present*, Anthropological Survey of India, Government of India, Calcutta, June 1978.

Ghurye, G.S., *Caste, Class and Occupation*, Popular Prakashan, Bombay, 1961.

— *Caste and Race in India*, Kegan Paul, London, 1932 and Popular Prakashan, Bombay, 1969.

Girling, D.A. (ed.), *Everyman's Encyclopedia*, 6th edn., J.M. Dent and Sons Ltd., London, 1978.

Grianembal, K., *Festivals of India*, Anthropological Survey of India, Government of India, Calcutta, 1969.

Gore, M.S., *Urbanization and Family Change*, Popular Prakashan, Bombay, 1968.

Gupta, A., *Indian Abroad: Asia and Africa*, (ed.), Orient Longman, Allahabad, 1971.

Gupta, Dipankar, *Social Stratification*, Oxford University Press, Bombay 1992.

Gupta, G.R. (ed.), *Family and Social Change in Modern India*, Vikas Publishing House Pvt. Ltd., Delhi, 1976.

— *Contemporary India: Some Sociological Perspective*, Vikas Publishing House Pvt. Ltd., Vol. I, Delhi, 1976.

Gupta, M.N., *भारत में सशस्त्र क्रान्ति चेष्टा के इतिहास*, Allahabad, 2nd Edition, 1946.

Halsey, William D., *Collier's Encyclopedia*, Vol. 7, Macmillan Educational Corporation, New York, 1977.

Hindlin, Oscar, *The Uprooted*, Grossett and Dunlop, New York, 1951.

Hitchocock, R.H., *A History of the Malabar Rebellion*, Government Press, Madras, 1925.

Issac, J., *Economics of Migration*, Kegan Paul, Trench and Trubner, London, 1947.

Jackson, J.A., (ed.), *Migration*, Cambridge: The University Press, 1969.

Jahode, et al., *Research Methods in Social Relations*, Henry Holt and Company, Inc., 1959.

Jayaraman, R., *Caste Continuities in Ceylon*, Popular Prakashan, Bombay, 1975.

Johnson, H.M., *Sociology: A Systematic Introduction*, Allied Publishing Pvt. Ltd., Third Indian Reprint, New Delhi, 1970.

Kapadia, K.M., *Marriage and Family in India*, Oxford University Press, Bombay, 1966.

Karve, I., *Kinship Organization in India*, Deccan College Research Institute, Poona, Asia Publishing House, Bombay, 1953.

Kloss, C. Boden, *Andamans and Nicobars*, Vivek Publishing House, Delhi, 1971.

Kosambi, *The Culture and Civilization of Ancient India in Historical Outline*, London: Routledge and Kegan Paul, 1965.

Kuper, Hilda, *Indian People in Natal*, Durban: Natal University Press, 1960.

Kiran, G. (ed.), *Family in India: A Regional View*, Mouton, The Hague, 1971.

Lal, Parmanand, *Andaman Islands: A Regional Geography*, Anthropological Survey of India, Government of India, Calcutta, March 1976.

Majumdar, R.C., *Penal Settlement in Andamans*, Gazetteers Unit, Department of Culture, Ministry of Education and Social Welfare, Government of India, New Delhi, 1975.

Man, Edward Horace, *Aboriginal Inhabitants of the Andaman Island*, Sanskaran Prakashan, Delhi, (Reprinted).

Mathur, L.P., *History of the Andaman and Nicobar Islands*, Sterling Publishers Pvt. Ltd., Delhi, 1968.

Mann, Peter H., *Methods of Sociological Enquiry*, Oxford: Basil Blackwell, 1968.

Mayer, Adrian C., *Land and Society in Malabar*, Oxford University Press, 1952.

— *Peasants in the Pacific: A Study of Fiji Indian Rural Society*, London, Routledge and Kegan Paul, 1961.

Mehta, S.R., *Social Developments in Mauritius*, Wiley Eastern Ltd., New Delhi, 1981.

Miller, R.E., *Mappila Muslims of Kerala*, New Delhi, Orient Longman, 1976.

Mines, M., *Muslim Merchants*, Shri Ram Centre for Industrial Relation and Human Resources, New Delhi, 1972.

Mishra, B.B., *The Indian Middle Class*, Oxford University Press, Bombay, 1961.

Morris, H.S., *The Indian of Uganda*, Chicago, University of Chicago Press, 1968.

Mouat, Fredric John, *Adventures and Researches Among the Andaman Islands*, London, 1963.

Mukherji, S.B., *Indian Minority in South Africa*, Peoples Publishing House, New Delhi, 1959.

Nepali, G.S., *The Newars*, United Asia, Bombay, 1965.

Portman, M.V., *A History of Our Relations with the Andamanese*, Vol. I and II, Calcutta, Office of the Supdt. of Government Printing.

Puthenkalam, Fr. J.S.J., 'The Mappillas of Malabars', in 'Marriage and the Family in Kerala', *Journal of Comparative Family Studies*, The University of Calgary, Canada, 1977.

Robson, L.L., *The Convict Settlers of Australia*, Australia, Melbourne University Press, 1965.

Saksena, R.N., *Sociology and Social Policy in India*, Orient Longmans, Calcutta, 1964.

Sandhu, K.S., *Indians in Malaya: Immigration and Settlement 1786-1957*, London, Cambridge University Press, 1969.

Sen, P.K., *Land and People of the Andamans*, The Post-Graduate Book Mart, Calcutta, 1962.

Shah, A.M., *The Households Dimension of the Family in India*, Orient Longmans Ltd., Delhi, 1971.

Shah, P.G., *The Dublas of Gujarat*, Bharatiya Adimjati, Sevak Sangh, Kingsway, Delhi, May 1958.

Singer and Cohen (ed.), *Structure and Change in Indian Society*, Aldine Publishing Co., Chicago, 1968.

Singh, Harijinder (ed.), *Caste Among Non-Hindus in India*, National Publishing House, New Delhi, 1977.

Singh, K.J.B., (ed.) *The Other India*, Arnold-Heinemann, New Delhi, 1979.

Singh, N. Iqbal, *The Andaman Story*, New Delhi: Vikas Publishing House Pvt. Ltd., 1978.

Singh, Y., *Modernization of Indian Tradition*, Thomson Press (India) Ltd., Delhi, 1972.

— *Caste and Class: Some Aspects of Continuity and Change, Sociological Bulletin*, Bombay, Vol. 27, 1968.

Srinivas, M.N., *Religion and Society among the Coorgs of South India*, Clarendon Press, Oxford, 1952.

— *Caste in Modern India and Other Essays*, Asia Publishing House, London, 1962.

Suryanarayan, V. and V. Sudarsen (eds.), *Andaman and Nicobar Islands: Challenges of Development*, Konark Publishers Private Limited, Delhi, 1994.

Sykes, Sir Percy M., *History of Exploration*, London: Routledge and Kegan Paul, 1950.

Tarachandra, *भारतीय स्वतन्त्रता आन्दोलन का इतिहास*, Publication Division, Ministry of Information and Broadcasting, Government of India, New Delhi, 1969.

Vaidya, S., *Islands of the Marigold Sun*, London: Robert Hale Ltd., 1960.

Whyte, William, *Street Corner Society*, University of Chicago Press, 1949.

Wiebe, Paul D., *Social Life in an Indian Slum*, Vikas Publishing House Pvt. Ltd., Delhi, 1975.

Wiebe, Paul D. and Mariappen, S., *Indian Malaysians*, Manohar: New Delhi, 1978.

Young, P.V., *Scientific Social Surveys and Research*, Prentice Hall of India Pvt. Ltd., New Delhi, 1977.

Published Articles

Abdulla, V., 'The Moplahs', *The Illustrated Weekly of India*, Bombay, February 1, 1970.

Bajpai, N., *हवाले पानी का सब्ज पत्थर*, *Kadambini*, February 1975, Delhi, pp. 154-159.

— *हवाले पानी का सब्ज पत्थर*, *Kadambini*, March 1976, Delhi, pp. 103-108.

— *पोर्टब्लेयर आँसू भरी कुछ यादें*, *Kadambini*, December 1975, Delhi, pp. 134-140.

Balakrishna, N.V., 'Moplah Rebellian', *Indian Review*, Madras, Vol. XXIII, April 1920, p. 105.

Bannings, J.J., 'The Mpolah Rebellian of 1921', *The Moselem World*, XIII (1923), pp. 317-89.

Barua, D.S., 'The Andaman Isles', *Imprint*, Vol. XV, No. 11, February 1976.

Dandekar, V.N., and Rath, N., 'Poverty in India', in *Economic and Political Weekly*, VI, January 2, 1971.

Ferrar, M.L., 'New Penal Settlement in Andamans', 1931, Society Arts, Vol. 80, pp. 48-61.

Hurshe, G.R.D., *पावन भूमि अण्डमान, स्वतन्त्रता का सिंहद्वार*, Government Press, Port Blair, 1979.

Joshi, A,K., स्वतन्त्रता सेनानियों की यातना भूमि, *साप्ताहिक हिन्दूस्तान*, New Delhi, September 16, 1984.

Joshua, Shirley, 'Andaman Rotting in the Sun', *India Today*, the Fortnightly News Magazine, Vol. III, No. 8, April 16-30, 1978.

Mallet, F.L., 'On Some of the Mineral Resources of the Andaman Islands in the Neighbourhood of Port Blair', Res. G.S.I., Vol. XVII, 1884.

Mitra, Manojit, 'A New Society', *The Statesman*, Monday, May 10, 1976, Calcutta.

Maidu, K.S., 'Mopilah Rebellion - 1921', *स्वतन्त्रता का सिंहद्वार*, Government Press, Port Blair, 1979.

Nambiar, A.K.P., 'Story of the Penal Settlement in the Bay Islands', *स्वतन्त्रता का सिंहद्वार*, Government Press, Port Blair, 1979.

Nityanandan, P.M., 'The Islander: A Story of the Andamans', *Imprint*, Vol. XV, No. 11, February 1975.

Patra, M.K., 'Socio-Econoic Linkage of Development: The People of Andaman and Nicobar Islands', Population Change and Rural Development of India, (ed.) J.R., Rele and M.K. Jain, International Institute for Population Studies, Deonar, Bombay, 1978.

Sharma, R.P., 'Assam-type Stir Grips Andamans', *Blitz*, November 8, 1980.

— 'काले पानी की महिला का संक्षिप्त इतिहास' *मनोरमा*, February, 55th Year, Issue 3, 1979.

Srivastava, P., 'In Face of Death – The Andaman Islands under Japanese Occupation from Match 1942 to Oct. 1945', *The Indian Archives*, Vol. XXVIII, Numbers 1-2, January-December 1979, New Delhi.

Published Reports of the Government of India

(a) *Census Report of the Andaman and Nicobars, 1901* by Sir Richard Temple.

(b) *Census Report, Andamans and Nicobars, 1911*, Vol. II by R.F. Lowis.

(c) *Census Report, Andamans and Nicobars, 1921*, Vol. II by R.F. Lowis.

(d) *Census Report, Andamans and Nicobars, 1931*, Vol. II by C.J. Bonnington.

(e) *Census Report, Andamans and Nicobars, 1951*, Vol. XVII by A.K. Ghosh.

(f) *Census Report, Andamans and Nicobars, 1961, 1971, 1981, 1991, 2001* (Provisional).

(g) 'The Imperial Gazetteer of India', Vol. XX, Oxford: The Clarendon Press, 1908.

(h) 'The Andaman and Nicobar Manual', Published by Authority, Calcutta, Supdt. of Government Printing, India, 1908.

(i) 'Imperial Gazetteer', Provincial Series, Andamans and Nicobars, Calcutta, 1907.

(j) 'Report on the Possibilities of Colonisation and Development of the A&N Island', 1949 by H.R. Shivdasani, Government of India, Ministry of Home Affair, New Delhi.

(k) 'The Andaman and Nicobar Information', 1962-1996.

(l) 'The Andaman and Nicobar Administration Annual Report', 1960-1996.

Other Published Report

(a) 'Techno-Economic Survey of Andaman and Nicobar Islands'; National Council of Applied Economic Research, New Delhi, July 1972.

Unpublished Records in the Custody of National Archives of India, New Delhi

(a) Indices and Proceedings of the Secret Department of the East India Company from 1764 to 1858.
(b) Indices and Proceedings of the Public, Judicial, Jails and Police Branch of the Home Department of the Government of India from 1858 to 1916.
(c) Indices and Proceedings of the Port Blair Branch of the Home Department of the Government of India from February 1873 to 1916.

Also Consulted

1. Weekly Newspaper of Port Blair "The Light of Andaman" (Editor Paras Ram), December 1979 to January 1981.
2. Daily Newspaper of Andaman and Nicobar Administration "The Daily Telegram", from December 1979 to January 1981.
3. "The Andaman Times", Newspaper of Port Blair, from December 1979 to January 1981.
4. Special Andaman issue of *Yojana*, Vol. XX/13, 15 August 1976.
5. Administrations Unpublished Report on "A Note on Ex-Serviceman Settlement at Great Nicobar and other Activities on that Island", 1978.
6. Administrations Unpublished Report on "A detailed note on the Rehabilitation Programme Being Implemented in Little Andaman", 1978.
7. Consulted various newspapers - *National Herald*, Delhi, 31 January 1974; *Indian Express*, Delhi, 30 June 1975; *Patriot*, 4 December 1977; *Times of India*, Delhi, 10 December 1977; *Amrita Bazar Patrika*, Calcutta, 27 February 1979; *Statesman*, Delhi, Times, 10 July; *Search Light*, Patna, 19 September 1976, and *Indian Express*, New Delhi, 9 May, 1976.

Index